M

Janice VanCleave's

A+
PROJECTS IN
ASTRONOMY

Janice VanCleave's

A+
PROJECTS IN
ASTRONOMY
Winning Experiments for
Science Fairs and Extra Credit

John Wiley & Sons, Inc.

ISBN 0-471-32820-0 (paper: alk. paper)
ISBN 0-471-32816-2 (cloth: alk. paper)

Printed in the United States of America

10 9 8 7 6 5 4 3 2 1

Dedication

It is a pleasure to dedicate this book to fellow amateur astronomers and members of the Central Texas Astronomical Society, Johnny Barton, Paul Derrick, and John W. McAnally.

Johnny is an officer of the astronomy club and has been an active amateur astronomer for more than 20 years. John is also on the staff of The Association of Lunar and Planetary Observers where he is acting Assistant Coordinator for Transit Timings of the Jupiter Section. Paul is the author of the "Stargazer" column in the *Waco Tribune-Herald*. These scientists have been invaluable resources for the information in this book.

Acknowledgments

Dr. Glenn S. Orton, a Senior Research Scientist at the Jet Propulsion Laboratory of the California Institute of Technology. Glenn is an astronomer and space scientist who specializes in investigating the structure and composition of planetary atmospheres. He is best known for his research on Jupiter and Saturn. I have enjoyed exchanging ideas with Glenn about experiments for modeling astronomy experiments.

Dr. Laura Barge, Senior Research Scientist, CASPER (Center for Astrophysics, Space Physics & Engineering Research). Laura has not only provided information about astronomy concepts, but she has introduced me to new ways of making learning about the heavens above us more fun.

A special note of gratitude to these educators who assisted by pretesting the activities and/or by providing scientific information: Holly Harris, China Spring Intermediate, China Spring, Texas; Laura Roberts, St. Matthews Elementary, Louisville, Kentucky; Dr. Tineke Berends Sexton, Biology Instructor at Houston Community College System; and Marsha Willis, Middle School Science Coordinator at Region 12 Educational Center, Waco, Texas. Marsha has not only assisted with reviewing activities for this but was instrumental in our being involved in NASA's Texas Fly High Program, which provided the opportunity for me to fly in NASA's Vomit Comet.

Contents

Part V   Moons

Part VI   Stars

Part VII   Meteors and Artificial Satellites

Introduction

Science is a search for answers to all kinds of interesting questions about our world. Science projects make excellent tools for you to use as you look for the answers to specific problems. This book will give you guidance and provide A+ project ideas. An A+ idea is not a guarantee that you will receive an A+ on your project. You must do your part by planning experiments, finding and recording information related to a problem, and organizing the data to find the answer.

Sharing your findings by presenting your project at science fairs will be a rewarding experience if you have properly prepared the exhibit. Trying to assemble a project overnight usually results in frustration, and you cheat yourself out of the fun of being a science detective. Solving a scientific mystery, like solving a detective mystery, requires that you plan well and carefully collect facts.

Start your project with curiosity and a desire to learn something new. Then proceed with purpose and a determination to solve the problem. It is likely that your scientific quest will end with some interesting answers.

Select a Topic

The 30 topics in this book suggest many possible problems to solve. Each topic has one "cookbook" experiment—follow the recipe, and the result is guaranteed. Read all of these easy experiments before choosing the topic you like best and want to know more about. Regardless of the problem you choose to solve, your discoveries will make you more knowledgeable about astronomy.

Each of the 30 sample projects begins with a brief summary of topics to be studied and objectives to be determined. Information relevant to the project is also included in the opening summary. Terms are defined when first used in the project, but definitions are not repeated throughout the text. Check the Glossary and/or Index to find explanations about any unfamiliar terms.

Try New Approaches

Following each of the 30 introductory experiments is a section titled "Try New Approaches" that provides additional questions about the problem presented. By making small changes to some part of the sample experiment, you achieve new results. Think about why these new results might have happened.

Design Your Own Experiment

In each chapter, the section titled "Design Your Own Experiment" allows you to create experiments to solve questions related to the sample problem. Your own experiment should follow the sample experiment's format and include a single statement of purpose; a list of necessary materials; a detailed step-by-step procedure; written results with diagrams, graphs, and charts, if they seem helpful; and a conclusion explaining why you got the results you did and answering the question you posed to yourself. To clarify your answer, include any information you found through research. When you design your own experiment, make sure to get adult approval if supplies or procedures other than those given in this book are used.

Get the Facts

Read about your topic in many books and magazines. You are more likely to have a successful project if you are well informed about the topic. For each topic in this book, the section titled "Get the Facts" provides some tips to guide you to specific sources of information. Keep a journal to record all the information you find from each source, including the author's name, the title of the book or article, the city of publication, the publisher's name, the year of publication, and the page numbers.

Keep a Journal

Purchase a bound notebook to serve as your journal. Write in it everything relating to the project. It should contain your original ideas as well as ideas you get from books or from people like teachers and scientists. It should also include descriptions of your experiments as well as diagrams, photographs, and written observations of all your results.

Every entry should be as neat as possible and dated. An orderly journal provides a complete and accurate record of your project from start to finish and can be used to write your project report. It is also proof of the time you spent sleuthing out the answers to the scientific mystery you undertook to solve. You will want to display the journal with your completed project.

Use the Scientific Method

Each project idea in this book will provide foundation material to guide you in planning what could be a prizewinning project. With your topic in mind and some background information, you are ready to demonstrate a scientific principle or to solve a scientific problem via the **scientific method.** This method of scientifically finding answers involves the following steps: research, purpose, hypothesis, experimentation, and conclusion.

Research: The process of collecting information about the topic being studied. It is listed as a first step because some research must be done first to formulate the purpose and hypothesis. Additional research will help you to explain your experimental results.

Purpose: A statement that expresses the problem or question for which you are seeking resolution. Once you have settled on an idea you want to investigate, turn it into a clear purpose statement.

Hypothesis: A guess about the answer to the problem based on knowledge and research you have done before beginning the project. It is most important to write down your hypothesis before beginning the project and not to change it even if experimentation proves you wrong.

Experimentation: The process of testing your hypothesis. Safety is of utmost importance. The projects in this book are designed to encourage you to learn more about astronomy by altering a known procedure, but please explore untested materials or procedures only with adult supervision or approval.

Conclusion: A summary of the experimental results and a statement that addresses how the results relate to the purpose of the experiment. Include explanations for experimental results that support or refute the hypothesis.

Assemble the Display

Keep in mind that while your display represents all that you have done, it must tell the story of the project in such a way that it attracts and holds the viewer's interest. So keep it simple. Try not to cram all your information into one place. To conserve space on the display and still exhibit all your work, keep some of the charts, graphs, pictures, and other materials in your journal instead of on the display board itself.

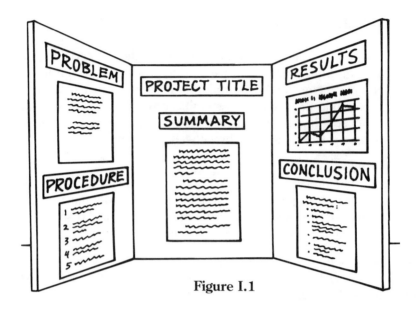

Figure I.1

The actual size and shape of displays vary according to local science fair official rules. Remember to check them out for your particular fair. Most exhibits are allowed to be 48 inches (122 cm) wide, 30 inches (76 cm) deep, and 108 inches (274 cm) high. Your display may be smaller than these maximum measurements. A three-sided backboard (see Figure I.1) is usually the best way to display your work. A cardboard or foam backboard can be purchased, or wooden panels can be hinged together, but you can also use sturdy cardboard pieces taped together to form a very inexpensive, but presentable, exhibit.

Your title should be placed at the top of the center panel. The title should be as short as possible and capture the theme of the project but not be the same as the problem statement. For example, suppose the problem under question is "Which stars are circumpolar?" An effective title might be "Around and Around: Locating Circumpolar Stars." The title and other headings should be neat and also large enough to be readable from a distance of about 3 feet (1 m). You can glue letters onto the backboard (buy precut letters or cut them out of construction paper) or use a computer to create them for all the titles. A short summary paragraph of about 100 words to explain the scientific principles involved is useful and can be printed under the title. Someone who has no knowledge of the topic should be able to easily understand the basic idea of the project just by reading the summary.

There are no set rules about the position of the information on the display. However, it all needs to be well organized, with the title and summary paragraph as the focal point at the top of the center panel and the remaining material placed neatly from left to right under specific headings. The headings you display will depend on how you wish to organize the information. Separate headings of "Problem," "Procedure," "Results," and "Conclusion" may be used.

Discuss the Project

The judges give points for how clearly you are able to discuss the project and explain its purpose, procedure, results, and conclusion. While the display should be organized so that it explains everything, your ability to discuss your project and answer the questions of the judges convinces them that you did the work and understand what you have done. Practice a speech in front of friends, and invite them to ask you questions. If you do not know the answer to a question, never guess or make up an answer or just say "I do not know." Instead, say that you did not discover that answer during your research, and then offer other information that you found of interest about the project. Be proud of the project, and approach the judges with enthusiasm about your work.

PART I

Measurements

Apparent Diameter: Observed Diameter of Celestial Bodies

1

Celestial bodies are natural objects in the sky, such as the Sun, moons, planets, and stars. The apparent diameter of a celestial body is not the actual diameter, but how large the diameter appears to be as viewed from Earth. Two objects of different actual diameters may have the same apparent diameter.

In this project, you will compare the apparent diameters of the Moon and the Sun and discover how their distances from Earth affect their apparent diameters. You will demonstrate and calculate the greatest and least distance ratios of the Sun and the Moon from Earth. You will determine a method of using the ratio of apparent diameter to apparent distance to determine the Moon's angular diameter, which is its apparent diameter measured in radians or degrees. You will also research different instruments of measuring angular size, such as the cross-staff and sextant.

Getting Started

Purpose: To determine how distance from Earth affects the apparent diameter of celestial bodies.

Materials

drawing compass
ruler
sheet of yellow
    construction paper
scissors
¼ inch (0.63 cm) one-hole paper punch

white index card
masking tape
yardstick (meterstick)
3 yards (3 m) of thin string

Procedure

1. Prepare a data table like Table 1.1.
2. Use the compass to draw a 1-inch (2.5-cm)-diameter circle on the yellow paper. Cut out the circle. Call this diameter D_1.

3. Use the paper punch to make a hole in the center near the edge of one short side of the index card. The diameter of the hole is ¼ or 0.25 inch (0.63 cm). Call it D_2.

4. Tape the yellow circle to a wall at eye level. A path of at least 3 yards (3 m) must be clear in front of the wall. Use tape to secure one end of the string to the center of the circle.

5. Thread the free end of the string through the hole in the index card.

6. Standing close to the wall, hold the bottom edge of the index card with both hands so that the hole in the card is at the top.

7. With your hands at arm's length in front of your face, stand so that the hole in the card is centered on the yellow circle.

8. Close one eye and look through the hole in the card with your open eye. As you continue to look through the hole, slowly back away from the yellow circle, letting the card move along the string. Stop when the outer edge of the yellow circle and the edge of the hole line up precisely.

9. In this position, continue to hold the card at arm's length with one hand and with the other hand pull the string taut between your open eye and the yellow circle.

10. Ask your helper to measure and record two distances: d_1, the length of the string from your face to the center of the yellow circle, and d_2, the length of the string from your face to the hole in the index card (see Figure 1.1). Record the distances in columns 4 and 5 of your data table for test 1.

Figure 1.1

11. The ratio of the diameters compared to the ratio of the distances is:

$$D_1/D_2 = d_1/d_2$$

- $D_1/D_2 = 1$ inch/0.25 in = 4/1 (2.5 cm/0.63 = 4/1)

- Use the distance measurements from step 10 to calculate the distance ratio, d_1/d_2, by dividing the numerator by the denominator. Record the distance ratio in column 7 of your data table for test 1.

12. Repeat steps 6 to 11 four times, recording the results for tests 2 to 5.

13. Average the distance measurements for d_1 and d_2. Record the averages in columns 4 and 5 of your data table.

14. Average the calculations for d_2/d_1. Record the average in column 7 of your data table.

Table 1.1 Distance/Diameter Data						
Test	Diameter, inches (cm)		Distance, inches (cm)		Diameter Ratio	Distance Ratio
	D_1	D_2	d_1	d_2	D_1/D_2	d_1/d_2
1	1 (2.5)	0.25 (0.63)			4/1	
2	1 (2.5)	0.25 (0.63)			4/1	
3	1 (2.5)	0.25 (0.63)			4/1	
4	1 (2.5)	0.25 (0.63)			4/1	
5	1 (2.5)	0.25 (0.63)			4/1	
Average	1 (2.5)	0.25 (0.63)			4/1	

Results

The ratio of the diameters and the ratio of the distances are both equal to or close to 4/1, or 4 to 1. Because these diameter and distance ratios are the same, the small hole appears to be the same size as the larger paper circle when viewed at a distance from the circle.

Why?

As you move away from the wall, the **apparent diameter** (how large an object's diameter appears to be from a specific distance) of the yellow circle decreases. Since the ratio of the diameter of the circle to that of the hole is 4 to 1, the yellow circle appears to be the same size as the hole in the card when the ratio of their distances from your eye is also 4 to 1. The same thing can be true of **celestial bodies,** which are natural objects in the sky such as the Sun and the Moon, when viewed from Earth. The ratio of the actual diameter of the Sun to that of the Moon is 400 to 1, and the average ratio of the distance of the Sun from Earth to that of the Moon is also approximately 400 to 1. Because the diameter of the Sun is about 400 times the diameter of the Moon, and because the Sun is also 400 times farther away from Earth than is the Moon, the Moon and the Sun have the same apparent diameter.

Try New Approaches

1a. Since the actual diameters of the Sun and the Moon don't change, their diameter ratio is always about 400 to 1. However, the distances of the Sun and the Moon from Earth do change somewhat. This is because Earth's orbit around the Sun and the Moon's orbit around Earth are not perfect circles. Instead they are slightly flattened circles called **ellipses** (see Figure 1.2). Therefore the distance ratio of the Sun and the Moon from Earth is sometimes more and sometimes less than 400 to 1. Determine how an increase in this distance ratio affects the apparent diameters of the Sun and the Moon. The distance ratio is greatest when Earth is at **aphelion** (point in a planet's orbit farthest from the Sun) and the Moon is at **perigee** (the orbital point of the Moon or man-made satellite at the least distance from Earth). To demonstrate this, stand so that d_1 and d_2 are at the average measurements in the experiment and bend your arm so that d_2 is shorter and d_1 is longer. Note how the yellow circle fits into the hole in the card.

b. The least distance ratio of the Sun and the Moon from Earth occurs when Earth is at **perihelion** (the point in a planet's orbit at the least distance from the Sun) and the Moon is at **apogee** (point in the Moon's or a man-made satellite's orbit farthest from Earth). To demonstrate this, repeat the previous experiment; turn slightly so that you extend your arm farther so that d_2 is longer and d_1 is shorter. Note how the yellow circle fits into the hole in the card.

2a. Calculate the greatest distance ratio of the Sun and the Moon from Earth. At aphelion, Earth is about 95 million miles (152 million km) from the Sun. When the Moon is at perigee, it is about 227,063 miles (363,300 km) from Earth.

b. Calculate the least distance ratio. At perihelion, Earth is 91.9 million miles (147 million km) from the Sun. When the Moon is at apogee, it is 253,437 miles (405,500 km) from Earth. **Science Fair
Hint:** Make a drawing like the one in Figure 1.2 to represent the
positions of Earth, the Moon, and the Sun at the greatest and least
distance ratios. Add your calculated distance ratios to your diagram.
Note that your diagram does not have to be drawn to scale and the
ellipses can be exaggerated for illustrative purposes. Do make a
note on your diagram explaining this.

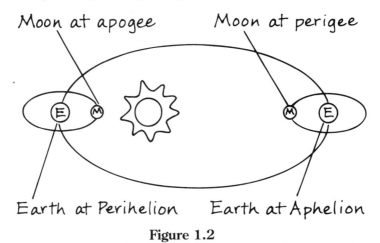

Figure 1.2

Design Your Own Experiment

1a. Design an experiment to demonstrate how the ratio of the apparent
diameter to the apparent distance of the Moon can be used to determine the Moon's **angular diameter** (apparent diameter, measured
in radians or degrees). One way is to cut a 2-inch (5-cm) -diameter
circle from an index card or other stiff paper to represent the Moon.
Call this diameter D_1. Tape the paper moon to a tree or other outdoor structure. Set a chair on the ground so that it faces the tree
with its back 19 feet (5.7 m) from the tree.

   Prepare a measuring instrument. First, cut a 1-by-2-inch (2.5-cm-
by-5-cm) piece from an index card. Using a paper punch, make a
hole in the center of the card. The diameter of the hole, ¼ inch (0.63
cm), is the apparent diameter of the paper circle (the Moon) and is
called D_2. Bend the card about ½ inch (1.25 cm) from one short end,
and tape the card to the zero end of a yardstick (meterstick). The
hole in the card should be just above the surface of the measuring

stick (see Figure 1.3). Rest the measuring stick on the back of the chair, aiming the end with the card toward the paper moon. Lay a pencil on the ground parallel to and 1 foot (30 cm) from the back of the chair.

Kneel by the pencil with the edge of the measuring stick next to one side of your face. Close one eye and use your open eye to look at the paper moon through the hole in the card. Keeping your head still, slide the measuring stick back and forth along the side of your face until the circle on the tree exactly fills the hole in the card. Record the measurement on the stick at the point even with your open eye as d_2. This is the apparent distance to the paper moon from an actual distance of 20 feet (6 m), which is d_1. Use the following equation to calculate the angular size(S), in degrees, of the paper moon:

$$S = 57.3° \times D_2/d_2$$

Figure 1.3

Note: D_2/d_2 yields a number without a unit of measurement. When no unit of measurement is indicated in giving the measure of an angle, the angle is understood to be expressed in radians. To express the angle in degrees, the conversion 57.3° per 1 radian is used.

Repeat the measurement four times and calculate an average. *Note:* Make sure D_2 and d_2 are expressed in the same units. For example, if D_2 is in inches, d_2 must be also.

b. In your demonstration, how does the ratio of actual diameter, D_1, to actual distance of the Moon, d_1, compare to the ratio of apparent diameter to apparent distance of the Moon, $D_1/d_1 = D_2/d_2$? Use the measurements to calculate each ratio by dividing the numerator by the denominator.

2a. During a full moon, use the instrument in the previous investigation to determine the angular diameter of the Moon. Take five measurements and, using the method in Appendix 1, determine your random error of measurement. **CAUTION:** *Do not attempt this experiment with the Sun, because looking at the Sun even for just a few seconds can cause permanent damage to your eyes.*

b. The angular diameter of the Moon varies from 0.49° at apogee to 0.55° at perigee. Using 0.5°, the average angular diameter of the full moon, the average angular diameter measured in the previous experiment, and the method in Appendix 2, calculate the relative error (also called percentage error) of your investigative results. What might account for any relative measuring error?

Get the Facts

The cross-staff and sextant are other instruments used to measure how large the angular measurement between two points appears to be, called the *angular distance* and angular diameter. Find out more about these instruments. For information, see the next project and also Richard Moeschl, *Exploring the Sky* (Chicago: Chicago Review Press, 1993), pp. 115–123.

Angular Separation: Angular Distance between Celestial Bodies

2

The apparent distance between celestial bodies is how large the linear measurement between bodies appears to be from Earth. Angular separation or angular distance is the apparent distance expressed in radians or degrees.

In this project, you will build a cross-staff resembling the instrument used by early navigators and astronomers. You will use it to measure both angular separation and angular diameter of celestial bodies including the Moon.

Getting Started

Purpose: To make and use a cross-staff to measure angular separation.

Materials

pen

white copy paper

scissors

stapler

yardstick (meterstick)

Procedure

1. Trace or photocopy the cross-staff pattern (see Figure 2.1).
2. Cut along the solid lines.
3. Fold the paper away from you along the dashed lines.
4. Position the T-shaped top so that its A and B sides meet the A and B sides of the bottom. Staple the A sides together first, then staple the B sides.
5. Slip the yardstick (meterstick) through the rectangular cutout section and between the top and bottom sections that are stapled together. The side labeled "W," "M," and "S" should face the zero end of the measuring stick. The paper is the crosspiece. It has a wide sight, "W," 4 inches (10 cm) across; a medium sight, "M," 2 inches (5 cm) across; and a small sight, "S," 1 inch (2.5 cm) across (see Figure 2.2). The notches in each side of the crosspiece are smaller sights and will be used in a later experiment.

16

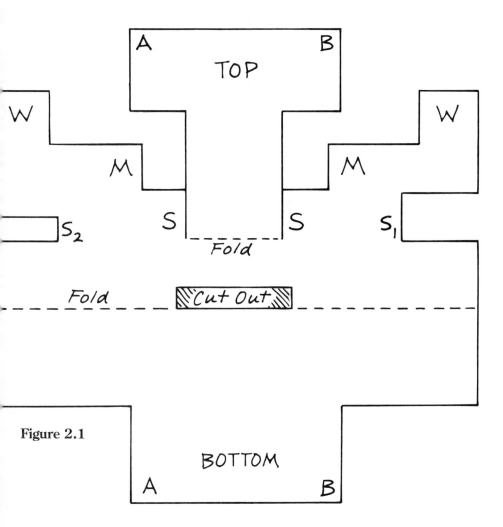

Figure 2.1

6. Use the cross-staff to measure angular separation. You can take measurements inside or outdoors.

- Stand 4 yards (4 m) from a closed door or other object. Record this sighting distance in column 1 of an Angular Separation (Wide Sight) Data table like Table 2.1.

- Rest the zero end of the measuring stick against one of your cheekbones. Close the eye over the cheekbone and use your open eye to sight along the length of the stick. Slide the crosspiece until the left side of the door lines up with the left-hand edge of the wide sight and the right side of the door lines up with the right-

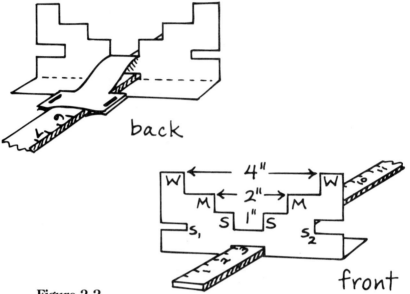

Figure 2.2

hand edge of the wide sight (see Figure 2.3). The width of the wide sight is d_1 and is equal to 4 inches (10 cm). Record this sight width in column 2 of your data table as shown.

- Read the value on the measuring stick where the bottom of the labeled side of the crosspiece touches the measuring stick. This measurement is d_2, the distance from the sight to your eye. Record measurement d_2 in column 3 of your data table for trial 1.

7. Repeat step 6 four times, for a total of five independent measurements of the same distance.

8. Calculate the angular separation between the left and right sides of the door in degrees, $0°$, using the average of your five measurements for d_2 and this equation:

$$D_a = 57.3° \times (d_1 \div d_2)$$

where D_a is the angular separation, d_1 is the width of the sight, and d_2 is the distance from the sight to your eye. D_a is expressed in degrees. Both d_1 and d_2 must be expressed in the same unit—either inches or centimeters. ***Note:*** $d_1 \div d_2$ yields a number without a unit of measurement. When no unit of measurement is indicated in giving the measure of an angle, the angle is understood to be expressed in radians. To express the angle in degrees, the conversion 57.3° per 1 radian is used.

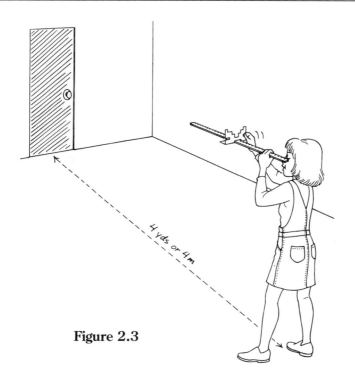

Figure 2.3

For example, for the wide sight, if d_1 = 4 inches (10 cm) and d_2 = 20 inches (50 cm), then

$$D = 57.3° \times 4 \text{ inches (10 cm)} \div 20 \text{ inches (50 cm)} = 11.45°$$

10. Using the method in Appendix 1, determine the measurement error. Record the error in column 10 of your data table.

Results

The angular separation will vary with door width. The author's measurement was 11.45°.

Table 2.1 Angular Separation (Wide Sight) Data								
Sighting Distance	Distance: Width of Sight (d_1), inches (cm)	Distance: Sight to Eye (d_2), inches (cm)					Angular Separation D_a,°	Error
		Trial 1	Trial 2	Trial 3	Trial 4	Trial 5	Average		
4 yards (4 m)	4 inches (10 cm)								

Why?

Like a circle, the sphere of sky surrounding Earth measures 360°. But only about half the sphere is visible above the **horizon** (imaginary line where the sky appears to touch Earth). So the sky you see covers an **arc** (segment of a circle) of about 180° from one side of the horizon to the other. As an observer from Earth, you look at celestial bodies from a great distance. The **apparent distance** between celestial bodies is how large the linear measurement between the bodies appears to be from Earth. The **angular separation** or **angular distance** is the apparent distance expressed in radians or degrees.

The **cross-staff** is an instrument used to determine angular separation. At a specific distance from an object, you measure the apparent width of an object (the width of the sight of the crosspiece) and the distance of the crosspiece from your eye. The ratio of apparent width to distance multiplied by 57.3° expresses the angular separation in degrees.

Try New Approaches

1a. Does the width of the cross-staff's sight affect the results? Repeat the experiment twice, using the medium, "M," and small, "S," sights. Compare your calculations.

b. Assess the accuracy of your cross-staff by determining the true angular separation between the sides of the door (D_A). Do this by using a ruler to measure the actual width of the door, d_a, and using the sighting distance, d_s, of 4 yards (4 m) and this equation:

$$D_A = 57.3° \times (d_a \div d_s)$$

For example, if door measurement d_a equals 29 inches, then

$$D_A = 57.3° \times (29 \text{ inches} \div 144 \text{ inches})$$
$$= 11.54°$$

c. Determine the relative error of your measurements using the method in Appendix 2.

2a. Does sighting distance (d_s) affect angular separation? Repeat the original experiment, collecting data for distances of 2, 4, 6, and 8 yards (m) using the wide sight. Determine the relative error for each sighting distance measurement.

b. Repeat the previous experiment using the medium and small sights of the cross-staff. Draw a line graph of your findings. Put the sighting distance on the horizontal axis. Put angular separation on the vertical axis. Use points and lines of different colors for the wide, medium, and small sights.

Design Your Own Experiment

1. Design an experiment to test the accuracy of the cross-staff in measuring angular separation between celestial bodies. For example, you might measure the angular separation of some of the stars in the Big Dipper, such as separation A shown in Figure 2.4 from Alkaid to Dubhe, separation B from Megrez to Dubhe, and separation C from Dubhe to Polaris. Record your measurements in a table like Table 2.2. If it is too dark to read your cross-staff, stand with the light from a building behind you. Make five measurements for each separation and average them. Compare your average with known angular separations given and record the difference. If the difference is more than the known value, record a positive (+) error. If the difference is less, record a negative (–) error. For more information about the angles between the stars of the Big Dipper, see Terence Dickinson, *Night Watch* (Willowdale, Ontario: Firefly Books, 1998), p. 30.

2. Design an experiment to determine if the angular separation of celestial bodies changes. Perhaps you can repeat the measurements between the stars of the Big Dipper at different times in one night or at the same time on different nights.

Table 2.2 Measuring Angular Separations with a Cross-Staff							
Location	Measured Angular Separation, °					Known Angular Separation,°	Error
	Trial 1	Trial 2	Trial 3	Trial 4	Trial 5	Average	
A							25°	
B							10°	
C							28°	

3. Use your cross-staff to measure the angular diameter of a celestial body such as the Moon. Since the Moon's diameter appears to be relatively small, use the smaller notch, S_2, on the left side of the crosspiece. If it is not a full moon, measure the Moon's height rather than its width. Compare this method with the method you used in Chapter 1, "Apparent Diameter."

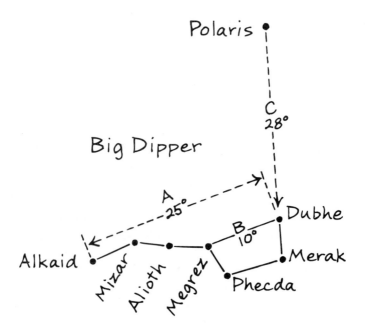

Figure 2.4

Get the Facts

The cross-staff was the first practical instrument for measuring the altitude of the Sun from the deck of a ship. The cross-staff measured the distance between the horizon and the Sun quite well, but it had problems. The user had to look directly at the Sun, risking eye damage or blindness. Another problem was aligning the crosspiece so that one end appeared to touch the Sun while the other touched the horizon. In 1594, John Davis (1550–1605), a British navigator, published his book *The Seaman's Secrets,* in which he described an improved instrument called the backstaff. What advantages did the backstaff have over the cross-staff? How were these two instruments different? For information about these and other navigational instruments, see Richard Moeschl, *Exploring the Sky* (Chicago: Chicago Review Press, 1993), pp. 115–123. Another resource is Dennis Fisher, *Latitude Hooks and Azmuth Rings: How to Build and Use 18 Traditional Navigational Instruments* (New York: TAB/McGraw-Hill, 1994).

3 Altitude: Vertical Coordinate

The celestial sphere is an imaginary sphere that has Earth at its center and on which all the other celestial bodies appear to be located. The altitude of celestial bodies above the horizon on the celestial sphere is measured in degrees, from 0° at the horizon to 90° at the zenith, the point directly overhead.

In this project, you will measure the approximate altitude of a star using your hands as the measuring tool. You will also use the angle of an object's shadow to determine the Sun's altitude.

Getting Started

Purpose: To measure the approximate altitude of a star.

Materials

your hands

Procedure

1. On a clear, moonless night, stand outdoors and select a bright star.

2. Use your hands and the method depicted in Figures 3.1 and 3.2 to measure the altitude of the star above the horizon. For example, if you measure a star at three fists and three fingers above the horizon, the star is at an altitude of about 35° above the horizon.

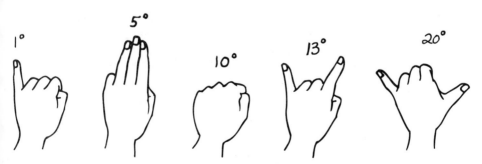

Figure 3.1

23

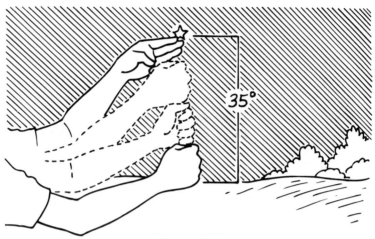

Figure 3.2

Results

The altitude of stars measured may vary. The one shown in the example is 35°.

Why?

A coordinate system called the **altazimuth system** is used in astronomy to locate celestial bodies by their **altitude** (angular height above the horizon) and **azimuth** (angular distance around the horizon). (See Chapter 4 for more information about the horizontal measurement of azimuth.) In describing this coordinate system, it is convenient to adopt the model of the **celestial sphere** (an imaginary sphere that has Earth at its center and all other celestial bodies scattered around the sphere). The **coordinates** (two numbers that identify a location) of altitude and azimuth are angles used to specify positions on the celestial sphere. In this experiment, the coordinate altitude is investigated. Altitude is a vertical measurement on the celestial sphere, measured in degrees above the horizon, from 0° at the horizon to 90° at the zenith. The width of different parts of your hand can be used to measure approximate altitudes of celestial bodies.

Try New Approaches

Altitude lines representing angular distances above the horizon can be imagined to form increasingly smaller, parallel circles from the horizon to the zenith of the celestial sphere. How do the lines of altitude compare to latitude lines. **Latitude lines** are imaginary parallel circles representing angular distances north and south of a celestial body's or the celestial sphere's **equator** (an imaginary line running east and west around the middle of a celestial body or the celestial sphere). On a clear, moonless night, face north and find the seven stars of the Big Dipper (see Figure 2.4 in Chapter 2). Follow the two stars in the bowl of the dipper to Polaris. Use your hands to measure the approximate altitude of Polaris above the horizon. Compare the altitude of Polaris to the latitude of your location on a map. Repeat this measurement at different latitudes, or ask friends who live in other parts of the country or world to take measurements for you. For more information about the comparison of celestial altitude and latitude lines, see *Janice VanCleave's Constellations for Every Kid* (New York: Wiley, 1997), pp. 64–72.

Design Your Own Experiment

1. Design an experiment to determine the altitude of the Sun without looking at the Sun. (Looking directly at the Sun can damage your eyes.) One way is to measure the shadow of an object cast by the Sun (see Figure 3.3). The object can be a dowel stuck vertically in the ground. Measure the length of the dowel above the ground and the length of the dowel's shadow at different times during the day. Use these measurements to find the **tangent** (in a right triangle, the ratio of the length of the side opposite an acute angle to the length of the angle's adjacent side). Then use the tangent table in Appendix 4 to find the angle. For example, if the dowel is 4 inches (10 cm) high, and its shadow is 11 inches (27.5 cm) long, the tangent (tan) of the Sun's altitude is:

$$\text{tan} = \text{height of dowel} \div \text{length of shadow}$$
$$= 4 \text{ inches } (10 \text{ cm}) \div 11 \text{ inches } (27.5 \text{ cm})$$
$$= 0.364$$

In the tangent table, the angle with a tangent of 0.364 is 20°. So the Sun's altitude is 20.0°. Prepare a table like Table 3.1 to represent this method.

Table 3.1 Determination of Sun's Altitude by Tangent					
Date	Time	Height of Dowel, inches (cm)	Length of Dowel's Shadow, inches (cm)	Tangent of Sun's Altitude	Sun's Altitude,°
June 3	10 A.M.	4 (10)	11 (27.5)	0.364	20.0

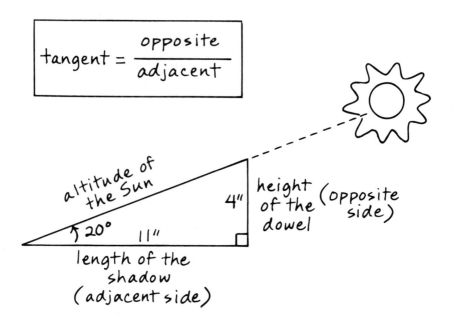

Figure 3.3

2. Design an experiment to represent the Sun's **diurnal motion** (apparent daily movement of a celestial body). One way is to use the altazimuth system, plotting the two coordinates, altitude and azimuth. Use the length of the dowel's shadow to determine the Sun's altitude. The azimuth of the Sun can be determined using the method in Chapter 4. Plot these two coordinates on a circle graph (see Figure 3.4). From measurements made during the day, you can **extrapolate** (make a logical estimate of the next value) the coordinates on the graph line to show the azimuth and altitude of the rising and setting Sun.

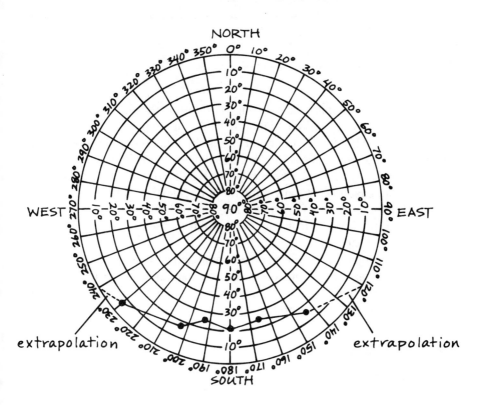

Figure 3.4

Get the Facts

In the Northern Hemisphere, the Sun is at its highest altitude on or about June 21 and at its lowest altitude on or about December 21. These times are called the *summer solstice* and *winter solstice,* respectively. How does Earth move in relation to the Sun to cause this apparent change in altitude? What and when are the equinoxes? For information, see *Janice VanCleave's Geography for Every Kid* (New York: Wiley, 1993), pp. 126–128.

4 | Azimuth: Horizontal Coordinate

An axis is an imaginary line through a body or the north-to-south line through the center of a celestial body from pole to pole about which the body rotates. One factor that determines the position of celestial bodies in the sky as seen from Earth is Earth's daily rotation, which is the turning of a body on its axis. This motion of Earth from west to east causes an apparent east-to-west daily movement of celestial bodies, such as the Sun, the Moon, stars, and planets. The angular distance measured eastward along the horizon from the north point on the horizon to a celestial body is called the azimuth.

In this project, you will make a simple astronomical measuring tool to determine azimuth. You will measure changes in the Sun's azimuth during one day and from day to day, and you will measure changes in the azimuth of other celestial bodies.

Getting Started

Purpose: To determine an azimuth of 0°.

Materials

premium-strength paper
    dinner plate
protractor
marking pen

grape-size piece of modeling clay
$^3/_{16}$-by-12-inch (0.47-by-30-cm)
    dowel
clock or watch

Procedure

1. Make a **compass rose** (a circle marked in degrees that is used to indicate azimuth) by turning the paper plate upside down. Then use the protractor and pen to mark every 10° around the edge of the paper plate as shown in Figure 4.1, starting with 0°. Label 0°N, 90°E, 180°S, and 270°W.

2. Use the clay to stand the dowel vertically in the center of the plate as shown in Figure 4.2.

3. At 30 minutes or more before noon standard time, set the plate outdoors in a sunny area and on a level surface. (**Standard time** is clock time disregarding daylight saving time.)

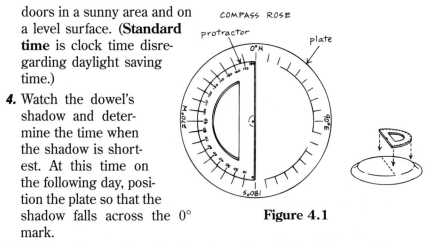

4. Watch the dowel's shadow and determine the time when the shadow is shortest. At this time on the following day, position the plate so that the shadow falls across the 0° mark.

Figure 4.1

5. Stand so that you face the direction of the shadow. You are facing an azimuth of 0°.

6. Imagine the shadow continuing until it touches the horizon. Make note of the physical structures at this point on the horizon.

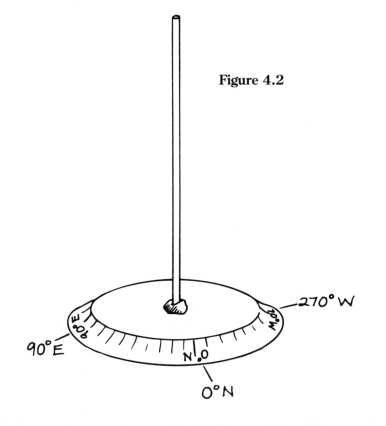

Figure 4.2

Results

You have determined the direction of an azimuth of 0° and identified physical structures on the horizon to mark this direction.

Why?

When the Sun is at its highest altitude in the sky, shadows are shortest. This time is called **high noon.** At high noon in the Northern Hemisphere, the Sun is at its highest position above the southern horizon. So the shadow of the dowel is cast toward an azimuth of 0°, which is **true north** (the direction of Earth's geographic North Pole, which is at the north end of Earth's axis).

The horizon makes a 360° circle. Each compass direction is 90° around the circle, so starting with 0° for true north and going eastward, true east is 90°, true south is 180°, and true west is 270°. The angular distance measured clockwise along the horizon from true north is called the azimuth. In this experiment, the dowel's shadow at high noon points to true north and leads to a point on the horizon with an azimuth of 0°. All celestial bodies on a line from the zenith to this point on the horizon have an azimuth of 0°.

Try New Approaches

1a. Once the azimuth of 0° (true north) is identified, other azimuth readings can be determined. With the 0° mark on the plate pointing toward azimuth 0°, true north, make note of structures along the horizon at the azimuth readings of 90° (east), 180° (south), and 270° (west).

b. Imaginary lines of azimuth extending from points on the horizon to the zenith can be used to measure the azimuth of celestial bodies at different altitudes. Use the structures noted in the previous experiment as markers to determine if the azimuth of stars changes during the night. Select four brighter stars in each of the four directions: north, east, south, and west. While standing in the same position, measure the azimuth of the four stars every 30 minutes for 2 or more hours. You can record a +, a −, or a 0 for an increase, a decrease, or no change, respectively in the azimuth, for each star. From your results, determine if there is any change in the azimuth of the stars and if so, if the change varies depending on where the star is located in the sky.

Design Your Own Experiment

1a. An **axis** is an imaginary line through a body or the north-to-south line through the center of a celestial body from pole to pole about which the body rotates. To an observer on Earth, the Sun appears to move across the sky because of Earth's **rotation,** which is the turning of a body on its axis. Design an experiment to measure the azimuth of the Sun over the course of a day without looking directly at the Sun. One way is to prepare a stationary compass rose. Do this by using a marker to draw a circle around the middle of two ⅜-by-8 inch (0.94-by-20-cm) dowels. Outdoors on a level section of ground, use a hammer to drive one of the dowels into the ground up to the mark. This will be dowel A. Save the second dowel for later. Use the marker and ruler to draw a line across the center of a 12-inch (30-cm)–square piece of thick corrugated cardboard. Label one end of the line "N" for north and the other end "S" for south. Use a drawing compass to draw a 6-inch (15-cm)–diameter circle in the center of the cardboard. Center the circle on the N-to-S line. Using the compass and a pen, mark every 5° clockwise around the circle as shown in Figure 4.3, starting at N. Label 0°N, 90°E, 180°S, and 270°W. You have drawn a compass rose.

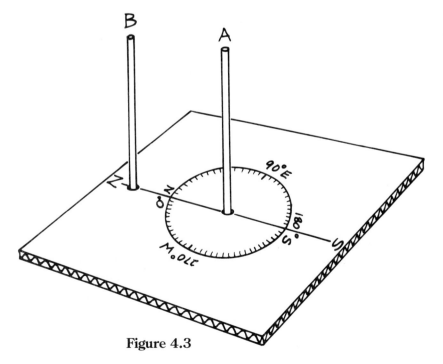

Figure 4.3

Use a nail to make two holes in the cardboard large enough for the dowels to easily slip through. Make one hole in the center of the circle and the other on the line and about 1 inch (2.5 cm) from the N. Slip the center hole in the cardboard over the dowel that is in the ground. Slide the cardboard to the ground. Turn the cardboard so that the north end of the line points in the direction of true north as determined in the original experiment. Insert the second dowel in the open hole in the cardboard. Use the hammer to drive the dowel into the ground up to the mark. This will be dowel B. In this position, the N points to true north. Remove the cardboard, leaving the dowels in place. **CAUTION:** *Cover each dowel with a bucket or a chair to prevent accidents.* The next day, at or near sunrise, put the cardboard back on the dowels. Determine where the first dowel's shadow crosses the compass rose.

The Sun's position is 180° from the direction of a shadow cast by the Sun. So, to determine the azimuth of the Sun at a particular time, subtract 180° from the azimuth of the dowel's shadow. For example, if the azimuth of the shadow is 300° the azimuth of the Sun is 300° − 180° = 120°. Take measurement of the azimuth of the dowel's shadow as often as possible, preferably every hour, between sunrise and sunset. In a table such as Table 4.1, record the time for each shadow measurement and the calculated azimuth of the Sun.

Table 4.1 The Sun's Diurnal Azimuth		
Time	Azimuth of Dowel's Shadow, °	Azimuth of the Sun, °
8:00 A.M.	300	120
9:00 A.M.		

b. From the information in the previous experiment, determine the **apparent speed** (angular distance per time) of the Sun across the sky during the day. Do this using the following formula.

speed = total change in azimuth ÷ total time

For example, if the first and last azimuth measurements are 110° at 8:00 A.M. and 240° at 6:00 P.M., respectively, the total change in azimuth would be 130° over a 10-hour time period. Thus, the apparent speed of the Sun would be 130° ÷ 10/hour = 13°/hour.

c. Does the apparent speed of the Sun change from day to day? Discover the answer by determining the daily speed of the Sun one or more days during a month for as many months as possible during one year. The longer you collect data, the more conclusive your results will be.

d. Is the azimuth of the Sun at sunrise and sunset the same each day of the year? Discover the answer by graphing the azimuth of the rising and setting Sun 1 day a week for as many weeks as possible during 1 year.

Get the Facts

Topocentric coordinates are also called *horizon* or *altazimuth coordinates*. One of the coordinates is the azimuth and the other the altitude. How do these coordinates compare for observers at different locations on Earth? For information see the *National Audubon Society Field Guide to the Night Sky* (New York: Knopf, 1991) pp. 64–66.

PART II

Optical Instruments

5 Apertures: The Gathering of Light

Many people credit the Italian astronomer and physicist Galileo (1564–1642) for inventing the telescope, which he built in 1609 and later improved. However, a Dutch spectacle maker, Hans Lippershey (c. 1570–c. 1619), is generally credited with the invention—in 1608. While Galileo most likely was not the first person to turn a telescope skyward to observe the heavens, he was the first to report his observations and made many new astronomical discoveries, such as the discovery in 1610 that Jupiter has moons. Many of Galileo's telescopes actually magnified less powerfully than today's inexpensive department store telescopes.

In this project, you will determine the function of the aperture of optical instruments. You will also investigate the three basic functions of optical instruments: light amplification (gathering light), magnification (increasing size), and resolution (enhancing clarity).

Getting Started

Purpose: To determine the function of the aperture of an optical instrument.

Materials

sheet of white copy paper	2 large bowls
ruler	yardstick (meterstick)
transparent tape	1-cup (250-ml) measuring cup
1 cup (250 ml) uncooked rice	helper

Procedure

1. Shape the paper into a cone with a 2-inch (5-cm) opening. Secure the cone with tape.

2. Place the rice in one of the bowls. Set the second, empty bowl on the ground outdoors.

3. With your helper holding the paper cone, open end up, over the empty bowl, hold the bowl of rice about 3 feet (1 m) above the cone and pour the rice into the cone (see Figure 5.1).

4. Use the measuring cup to determine the amount of rice that collects in the cone. Record the results in a Cone Capacity Data table like Table 5.1.

5. Repeat steps 2 to 4 four more times. Average the results and record the average in your data table.

Figure 5.1

Table 5.1 Cone Capacity Data						
Cone Size	**Rice Collected, cups (ml)**					
	Trial 1	Trial 2	Trial 3	Trial 4	Trial 5	Average
2 inches (5 cm)						

Results

Some of the grains of rice collect in the cone, while others fall outside the cone and into the bowl.

Why?

An **optical instrument** is a device that increases the power of human vision. The most commonly used examples are eyeglasses and contact lenses. Two other examples are binoculars and telescopes. Both binoculars and telescopes magnify objects viewed from a great distance, such as celestial bodies. The two main types of telescopes are the **refracting telescope,** which uses only lenses, and the **reflecting telescope,** which uses mirrors and lenses. **Binoculars** are somewhat like two small refracting telescopes joined together. But a refracting telescope produces an inverted image while prisms in binoculars change this to an upright image. The **objective lens** of a refracting telescope and the **primary mirror** of a reflecting telescope face the observed object and collect the light. The **aperture** of an optical instrument is the opening through which light enters. The size of the aperture of a telescope is the diameter of the objective lens or primary mirror.

In this investigation, the opening of the cone is like the aperture of a telescope, which gathers light. Each rice grain represents a **photon** (smallest particle of light). An aperture of a certain size can only gather a finite (limited) amount of light.

Try New Approaches

1a. Show how aperture size affects **light-gathering power** (the amount of photons that can be collected by an optical instrument). Repeat the investigation twice, first using a cone opening with a smaller diameter of 1 inch (2.5 cm), then a larger diameter of 4 inches (10 cm).

b. The light-gathering power of optical instruments can be compared by comparing the area of each aperture. Since the apertures of optical instruments are circular, the area of the aperture is equal to $\pi(d/2)^2$. Since π is the multiple used in determining the area of each aperture, and each diameter is divided by 2 to determine the radius, both π and 2 can be dropped from the equation. So the light-gathering power of two telescopes can be expressed as the ratio of the square of the diameter of their apertures. For example, to compare the light-gathering power of a 5-centimeter aperture to that of a 10-centimeter aperture, use this equation:

$$10^2/5^2 = 100/25 = 4/1$$

This means the 10-cm aperture will gather four times more light than the 5-cm aperture. Using the diameters of the openings in each cone, mathematically compare their light-gathering power. How does this compare with the amount of rice (photons) collected by each cone? For more information about light-gathering power, see Gregory L. Matloff, *Telescope Power* (New York: Wiley, 1993), pp. 28–29.

Design Your Own Experiment

1a. The light-gathering power of optical instruments results in **light amplification** (the process by which objects viewed through an optical instrument appear brighter than when viewed with the unaided eye). As the aperture of an optical instrument increases, its light-gathering power and thus its light amplification increases. The pupil of your eye is a variable aperture. In the light, your eye is said to become **light adapted** as a result of the contraction of the pupil, which decreases the eye's light-gathering power. In the dark, your eye becomes **dark adapted** as a result of the dilation of your pupil, which increases the light-gathering power of your eye. Design an experiment to show how much more light enters an optical instrument with a 2-inch (5-cm) aperture than enters the aperture of a dark-adapted eye dilated to a diameter of ¼ inch (0.63 cm). One way is to use ¼ inch (0.63-cm) holes made with a paper punch to represent the aperture of a dark-adapted pupil. Glue the punch-outs inside a 2-inch (5-cm)–diameter circle. How many can you fit? What does this tell you about the ability of a telescope to gather light? Using the number of circles, determine how many times brighter objects in the sky will appear when viewed with a 2-inch (5-cm) telescope than with your unaided, dark-adapted eye.

b. Use the equation $2^2/0.25^2 = ?/1$ to determine the exact light-gathering comparison of the 2-inch aperture with a dark-adapted eye.

2. All telescopes and binoculars contain lenses. The lens you look through is called the **eyepiece.** The lens at the opposite end of a refracting telescope or binoculars is called the objective lens or **objective.** (In reflecting telescopes, the objective is a mirror rather than a lens.) The focal length of a lens determines its magnification. **Magnification** is the enlargement of an image that can be determined by the ratio of the size of an object's image to the size of the object. **Focal length** is the distance from the lens to the **focal point,** the point where light rays passing through the lens **converge** (come together). Design an experiment to confirm that the focal length of a lens affects its magnification. One way to compare the focal length of a lens to its magnification is to measure the focal length of two or more magnifying lenses with different magnification. You can measure the approximate focal length by taping a white index card to the zero end of a yardstick (meterstick) so that the card is perpendicular to and even with the end of the measuring stick. Hold one magnifying lens with your writing hand. Support the card and ruler with your other hand and lay the free end of the measuring stick on the shoulder of your writing hand (see Figure 5.2). During the daytime, stand in a darkened room with your back to an uncovered window. Hold the magnifying lens on the measuring stick and move it toward and away from the index card until the brightest and clearest picture of the scene outside the window forms on the paper. Note the distance between the magnifying lens and the paper. This distance is slightly more than the focal length, and thus is the approximate focal length of the lens. Repeat, using a different lens.

Figure 5.2

3. The **magnifying power** of a lens is the number of times it can make the size of the image greater than the size of the object. Magnifying power of a lens is equal to the ratio of the average distance of distinct vision of most people, which is 10 inches (25 cm) to the focal length of the lens. This relationship is expressed as:

magnifying power = average distance of distinct vision/focal length

For example, if the focal length of a lens is 2 inches (5 cm), its magnifying power is:

magnifying power = 10 inches (25 cm) /2 inches (5 cm)
                  = 5/1 or 5×

This means that a 5× lens will magnify an object so that it appears five times the size it would appear if viewed at 10 inches (25 cm) with the unaided eye. Using this information, determine the magnifying power of the lenses used in the previous experiment.

Get the Facts

1. Since most celestial bodies are very faint, the light-gathering power of a telescope is its most important feature. With the best conditions, you can see a few thousand stars with your naked eye. Due to the light-gathering power of a telescope, even a telescope with a small aperture allows you to see a few hundred thousand stars. Compare the light-gathering power of some of the large telescopes, such as those at Kitt Peak, Mt. Palomar, and Yerkes.

2. The magnifying power of a telescope depends on the focal length of the objective and eyepiece. How is the magnifying power of a telescope calculated? How does the size of the objective focal length affect the magnifying power? For information, see "magnifying power" in the astronomy text.

3. The *resolution* of an optical instrument is a measure of image clarity. How do resolution and aperture relate? How do resolution and magnification relate? For more information, see Matloff, *Telescope Power,* pp. 32–33.

6 Diffraction: The Spreading of Light

Light is a form of radiation. Radiation is energy that travels through space in waves that have both electrical and magnetic properties. Energy emitted by stars contains several different forms of radiation, including visible light. Visible light is a part of the electromagnetic spectrum with different colors corresponding to different wavelengths, which is the distance from the point on one wave to the same point on the next.

Diffraction is one of the ways light is affected when it passes through a small opening. In this project, you will determine how diffraction hinders resolution, which is the ability of a telescope to separate the light of adjacent (nearby) stars and the importance of the resolving power of an optical instrument. You will also make and use a spectroscope to view the light spectrum.

Getting Started

Purpose: To observe diffraction of light.

Materials

straight pin

index card

pen

yardstick (meterstick)

desk lamp (with a visible light-bulb)

Procedure

1. Use the pin to make a tiny hole centered near the edge of one short end of the index card.

2. Circle the hole so you know where it is.

3. Fold the index card in half with the short ends together.

4. Partially unfold the card so that the two halves are at right angles to each other.

5. Hold the unmarked end of the card at the end of your nose. You should be able to see the circle you marked.

6. Close one eye. From 6 feet (1.8 m) or more, look through the pinhole at the illuminated bulb of the desk lamp (see Figure 6.1).

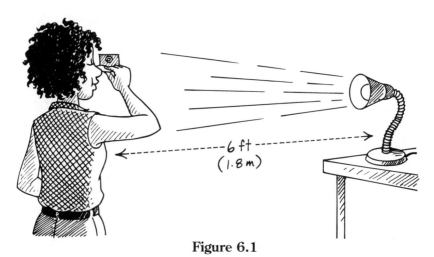

Figure 6.1

7. Observe the appearance inside the hole.

Results

Dark lines appear in the hole.

Why?

Diffraction is the spreading of light as it passes the edge of an obstacle and the blurred edges of the obstacle is called **diffraction fringe.** In this demonstration, some of the light passes directly through the center of the hole, but light hitting the edge of the hole bends (changes direction). Each point on the edge of the hole acts as a source of light. Where light rays from the sources meet, light and dark bands are formed. Think of light as a **wave,** which is a periodic disturbance in a substance or space that has **crests** (tops) and **troughs** (bottoms), as shown in Figure 6.2. When two waves meet, their crests and troughs overlap and the waves combine. If the crests and troughs match, the combined wave has crests and troughs with a greater **amplitude** (height). This is called **constructive interference.** The light produced is brighter and light bands are formed. But if the crests and troughs are opposite, the combined wave has less amplitude. This is called **destructive interference.** The light produced is less bright and can even be totally canceled out if the crests and troughs of the two waves are the same amplitude. Where the light is canceled, dark bands are seen. Despite the name, interference has no effect on the waves. After meeting, they continue to move forward as they did before the encounter.

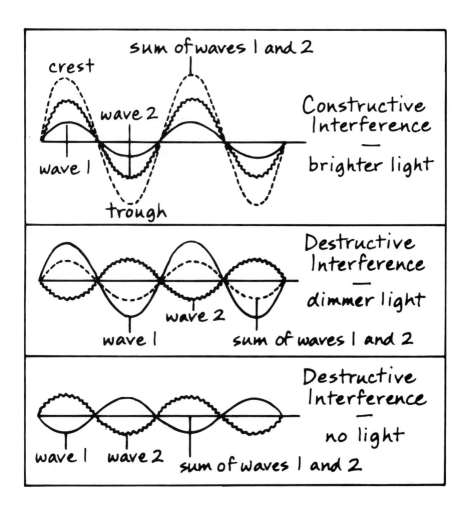

Figure 6.2

Try New Approaches

1a. Resolution is the capacity of an optical instrument to distinguish between two separate but adjacent light sources. The **resolving power** of a telescope is a measure of resolution and relates to the amount of diffraction fringe (blurred edge) around the image produced by the optical instrument. The better the resolving power, the less diffraction fringe and the clearer the image. Light from two stars that appear close to each other may overlap and appear as one star when viewed through a telescope with low resolving power. Demonstrate this by making a second hole in the card as close as possible to the first one. Repeat the experiment and observe how the light passing through the holes is **unresolved** (not separated).

b. How does the size of a telescope affect diffraction? Find out by making a hole about the size of a pencil point in an index card. Make several other holes that are even smaller. Repeat the original experiment, comparing the amount of interference in each hole. The clearer the light that passes through the hole, the less diffraction, the less interference, and the greater the resolution. From your results, determine which would produce better resolution, a telescope with a large or small lens or mirror?

Design Your Own Experiment

1a. Diffraction hinders viewing the stars through a telescope. But diffraction also helps separate light into its different wavelengths. A **spectroscope** is a device that breaks light into its component parts. Below are steps for building one. For more information, see Philip Harrington, *Astronomy for All Ages* (Old Saybrook, CT: Globe Pequot Press, 1994), pp. 178–179.

- Cover the end of a paper towel tube with aluminum foil.
- With adult approval, use a knife to cut a narrow slit in the aluminum foil cover.
- Cover the open end of the tube with a diffraction grating and secure the grating with tape. (Purchase a diffraction grating at a science novelty store or a science supply company. See Appendix 5.)
- Close one eye and look through the grating with your other eye. Point the hole in the tube toward the sky. **CAUTION:** *Do not aim the grating at or near the Sun because it can permanently damage your eyes.* Observe the colors that the light breaks into. These colors are called the **visible spectrum.** These colors, all together, make up white light. Consult a physical science or physics textbook for more information.

b. How does the light source affect the spectra produced? Discover this by using your spectroscope to look at different lights, such as a candle flame, an incandescent light, a fluorescent light, and a neon light.

Get the Facts

1. The different types of spectra include continuous, emission, bright-line emission, and dark-line emission. To learn more about the differences between spectra, see Brian Jones, *The Practical Astronomer* (New York: Fireside Books, 1990), pp. 42–43.

2. The spectra of light from stars vary in the brightness of some colors. They also differ in the number and arrangement of dark lines caused by destructive interference. How can dark spectral lines reveal whether the star is moving toward or away from Earth? To find out, see Robin Kerrod, *The Star Guide: Learning How to Read the Night Sky Star by Star* (New York: Macmillan, 1993), pp. 70–71.

PART III

The Sun

7 | Sunspots: Cooler Surface Regions

In the early 1600s in Paris, a German astronomer and Jesuit priest, Christoph Scheiner (1573–1650), was convinced he saw dark spots on the Sun. He was criticized for that idea because the renowned Greek philosopher Aristotle (384–322 B.C.) had stated that everything in the universe except Earth was perfect and without flaws. Scheiner revised his opinion and stated that the spots were caused by something near but not on the Sun. However, Galileo (1564–1642), an Italian scientist, saw the sunspots, studied their motion, and argued that they originated on the Sun. He is often credited as the first to discover them.

In this project, you will investigate the layers of the Sun. You will discover the photosphere, the area that appears to be the Sun's surface. You will observe the movement of sunspots to confirm that the Sun rotates. You will also learn how sunspots cycle and how they affect the Sun's activity.

Getting Started

Purpose: To build a model of the Sun's internal structure.

Materials

serrated knife (use with adult approval)

Styrofoam ball, 6 inches (15 cm) in diameter or larger

2 different colored permanent markers

four 1-by-4-inch (2.5-by-10-cm) white labels

4 round toothpicks

pen

Procedure

1. Use the knife to cut away one-fourth of the Styrofoam ball. Set the ball aside.

2. With one of the markers, paint an area in the center of the ball to represent the Sun's core.

3. Use the second marker to draw a band surrounding the core to represent the convection zone.

4. Prepare four flags using these steps:

- Touch the two sticky ends of a label together, leaving a gap near the folded end.
- Insert a toothpick through the gap and press the label on the tooth-pick to make a flag (see Figure 7.1).

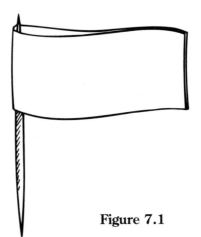

Figure 7.1

- Write the names of the Sun's layers on the flags: Photosphere, Convection Zone, Radiation Zone, Core.

5. Stick the flags in the Sun model as shown in Figure 7.2.

6. Make a Layers of the Sun table like Table 7.1, showing the thickness and temperature of each layer.

Table 7.1 Layers of the Sun		
Layer	**Thickness, miles (km)**	**Temperature, °F (°C)**
Core	87,000 (139,200)	27,000,032 (15,000,000)
Radiation Zone	239,250 (382,800)	4,500,032 (2,500,000)
Convection Zone	108,750 (174,000)	1,980,032 (1,100,000)
Photosphere	342 (547)	9,932 (5,500)

Results

You have made a model showing the layers of the Sun and a table describing some of their characteristics.

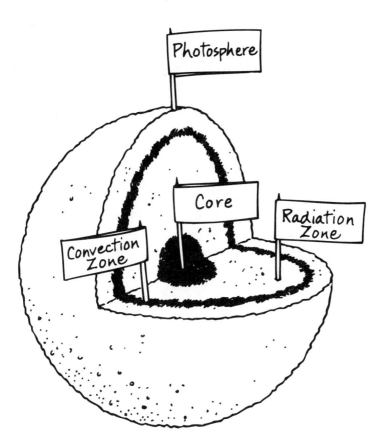

Figure 7.2

Why?

The Sun's **core** (center of a celestial body) is its hottest part. In the core, **nuclear fusion** (the combining of the nuclei of atoms) releases enormous amounts of **radiation** (energy that is transferred by electromagnetic waves, which have both magnetic and electrical properties). Energy from the hot core moves through the area outside the core called the **radiation zone.** From there, gases expand and rise. When they cool, they become denser and sink back down again. Circulating gas forms the **convection zone.** The next layer, the **photosphere,** is actually the first layer of the Sun's atmosphere. But from Earth, it looks like the Sun's surface. Your model does not show the layers of the atmosphere above the photosphere: the **chromosphere** and the outermost layer, the **corona.**

Try New Approaches

Photographs of the Sun's photosphere show that it has a grainy appearance called **granulation.** Covering the photosphere are bright spots resembling rice grains, called **granules.** A granule is the top of a rising current of hot gases from the convection zone. A single granule measures about 900 miles (nearly 1,500 km) across. Between the granules lie dark **intergranular lanes** where the cooler gases return to the convection zone. Also seen on the photosphere are large dark spots called **sunspots.** These are centers of intense localized magnetic fields that are thought to suppress the currents of hot gases. They are dark because they are cooler than the areas surrounding them. Find out more about granules and sunspots and add them to your Sun model. For information about the size of sunspots and their two observable regions, the **umbra** (darkest part) and the **penumbra** (grayish outer part), see Dinah Moche, *Astronomy: A Self-Teaching Guide* (New York: Wiley, 1996), pp. 102–105.

Design Your Own Experiment

The Sun rotates about once every 4 weeks. Design an experiment to confirm that the Sun rotates. Observe and record the location of sunspots over a period of time, but unlike Galileo, who looked directly at the Sun and in time lost his eyesight, *you must not look directly at the Sun.* A safe, indirect method of observing sunspots uses a telescope, but binoculars with one lens covered will work too. *Without looking through the lens,* point the telescope at the Sun and adjust the position of the instrument until its shadow is as small as possible. Then focus the Sun's image on a sheet of white poster board—the screen. Secure the telescope and screen so that they do not move by setting the telescope on a tripod and tacking the screen to a tree (see Figure 7.3). Cut a hole in a second piece of poster board large enough to fit around the end of the telescope that faces the Sun. This sheet of poster board casts a shadow on the screen, making the Sun's image easier to see. At the same time each day or as many days as possible for 2 weeks or more, tape a clean sheet of tracing paper to the screen. Mark the location of sunspots on the paper. Compare the drawings. How much do the sunspots move? Do some move faster than others? Does the path of sunspots reveal the location of the Sun's equator and poles? For more information, see Philip Harrington, *Astronomy for All Ages* (Old Saybrook, CT: Globe Pequot Press, 1994), pp. 77–79. **CAUTION:** *Never look directly at the Sun. It can permanently damage your eyes.*

Figure 7.3

Get the Facts

At any given moment, the number of visible sunspots can vary from several hundred to none at all. The number increases and decreases in a regular pattern called the *sunspot cycle*. How long does each cycle last? How does the Sun's activity relate to the number of sunspots? Get today's sunspot number at www.spaceweather.com. For more information, see Moche, *Astronomy,* p. 103.

8 True Sun: How the Sun Appears to Move

Planets orbit the Sun, which means they move in a curved path about the Sun. But planets do not orbit at uniform velocity. Because of the elliptical shape of Earth's orbit, Earth moves faster at perihelion and slower at aphelion. This difference in Earth's orbital velocities (speed of an object in a specific direction) makes the Sun appear to move at different speeds at different times.

In this project, you will model the Sun's apparent changes in **velocity.** You will compare true sun time or solar time with mean sun time or standard time. You will also learn about the analemma and how it can be used to predict time.

Getting Started

Purpose: To demonstrate the Sun's apparent motion when Earth is at aphelion.

Materials
outdoor tree

Procedure
1. Stand with your back to the tree (see Figure 8.1).

2. Walk forward eight paces.

3. Turn and slowly walk counterclockwise around one-fourth of the trunk of the tree.

4. As you walk, watch the tree trunk while also observing objects in the background.

Results
The tree appeared to move slowly against a background of stationary objects.

Figure 8.1

Why?

Astronomers have designed an imaginary sphere called the celestial sphere to help locate celestial bodies. Earth is pictured at the center of this large, hollow sphere, with all other celestial bodies, including the Sun, stuck on the inside surface of the sphere. From Earth, it appears that the Sun moves eastward among the stars across the surface of the celestial sphere. The apparent yearly path of the Sun across the celestial sphere is called the **ecliptic.**

In this investigation, you represented Earth, the tree represented the Sun, and the objects beyond the tree represented the celestial bodies, mostly stars, around the ecliptic. The path you walked was Earth's **orbit** (curved path around the sun). The apparent motion of the tree is really a reflection of how quickly you moved around it. This is also true for the apparent annual movement of the Sun, which is really a reflection of how quickly Earth **orbits** (moves in a curved path around) the Sun. Earth's orbital velocity (speed of an object in a specific direction) varies with its distance from the Sun. In early July, when Earth is at aphelion (farthest from the Sun), indicated by the eight paces, Earth moves slowest and the Sun moves slowest against the background of stars.

Try New Approaches

In early January, when Earth is at perihelion (closest to the Sun), Earth moves fastest and the Sun moves fastest against the stars. **True sun time** or **solar time** reflects this apparent change in velocity of the Sun during the year and is determined by the apparent position of the Sun in the sky. Thus, **solar noon** is the time when the Sun is at its highest altitude and hence casts the shortest shadows. Demonstrate Earth's motion at perihelion by respeating the experiment at six paces from the tree and walking quickly around the tree.

Design Your Own Experiment

1a. **Mean solar time** or standard time (also called **mean sun time**), representing a calculated average of the apparent motion of the Sun across the sky, is the same as clock time (disregarding daylight saving time). This time is based on the average or mean daily apparent distance the Sun travels, which is 1° per day eastward along the ecliptic. Design an experiment to compare solar time with standard time, in other words, to compare true sun time with mean sun time. One way is to use the shadow of a stick to determine solar noon and compare this with **standard noon** (12:00 P.M.). **Solar noon** is the time when the Sun is on the **meridian** (imaginary line drawn from north to south on the celestial sphere and passing through the zenith of the observer). Determine solar noon by following these steps:

- Draw a line down the center of the widest surface of a board that measures about 20 by 4 by 8 inches (5 by 10 by 20 cm) or larger. Label one end of the line "S" and the other end "N."

- On the line about 1 inch (2.5 cm) from the S end, hammer a long nail partway into the board. This nail must be perpendicular to the board.

- About an hour or more before standard noon (12:00 P.M. mean solar time), set the board outdoors on a flat surface. *Note:* Subtract an hour from your clock time during daylight saving time.

- Watch the nail's shadow as it gradually decreases in length. Record the clock time at solar noon, which is when the shadow is shortest. On the following day at this time, position the board so that the nail's shadow is aligned with the line between N and S. Record the date and clock time in a Solar Time vs. Standard Time Data table like Table 8.1. With the board in this position, the nail's shadow points toward true north and the time is solar noon.

- The N points toward true north, but it does not necessarily point **due north** (the direction of Earth's magnetic north pole). So that you can use a compass to find true north on other dates, find the compass direction of the shadow when it is pointed toward true north (see Figure 8.2).

Figure 8.2

- Once a week or more often, go outdoors one or more hours before standard noon (12:00 P.M. mean solar time) and set the board in the same place. Using the compass direction determined for true north, position the board so that N points to true north.

- In the data table, record the date and standard time when the nail's shadow aligns with the N-to-S line on the board, thus marking the moment of solar noon.

- Calculate the number of minutes solar time (true sun time) is ahead of or behind standard time (mean sun time). Do this by subtracting the clock time at solar noon from the clock time at standard noon, which is 12:00 P.M. For example, if solar noon is at 12:03, the difference would be 12:00 – 12:03 = –:03 or –3 minutes. This means that the Sun crosses the meridian at 12:03, 3 minutes later than the clock time at standard noon.

- Use a plus (+) to indicate true sun time is ahead and a minus (–) to indicate it is behind. The data chart shown here includes only two measurements, one when the Sun is behind and the other when the Sun is ahead of standard time.

Table 8.1 Solar Time vs. Standard Time Data		
Date	Clock Time at Solar Noon	Difference between Solar Noon Time and Standard Noon Time, Ahead (+), Behind (–)
Jan 1	12:03 P.M.	–3
May 11	11:56 A.M.	+4

b. If you start the observations when the Sun is not on the meridian, follow these steps to find true north.

- About 20 minutes before standard noon time, set the board on a level surface.

- Observe the nail's shadow. When it is as small as possible, position the board to align the shadow with the N-to-S line on the board. In this position, the shadow points toward true north.

Get the Facts

1. An *analemma* is an elongated figure eight. It shows the changing position of the Sun in the sky depending on the time of year. The analemma results from the alternately slow and fast travel of the Sun. How can it disclose the difference between true sun time and mean time? To find out, see Philip Harrington, *Astronomy for All Ages* (Old Saybrook, CT: Globe Pequot Press, 1994), pp. 89–95.

2. Today, the fame of German astronomer Johannes Kepler (1571–1630) mainly rests on his laws of planetary motion. In 1609 he described what is now called Kepler's second law of planetary motion, which is the law of equal areas. This law states that the orbital velocities of planets are not uniform, but vary in a regular way. How does the distance of a planet from the Sun affect its velocity? See an astronomy text for more information about Kepler's second law. You may wish to use a diagram to represent this law, showing that a line from a planet to the Sun sweeps out equal areas in equal times.

9 Seasons: Four Times of the Year

Seasons are regularly recurring periods of the year characterized by a specific type of weather. The four seasons are winter, spring, summer, fall. During the year the length of daylight and darkness varies from day to day. The longest period of daylight occurs on the first day of summer, and the shortest on the first day of winter. In the Northern Hemisphere, summer starts on or about June 21 and winter starts on or about December 22. These dates are called summer and winter solstices, respectively. On or about March 21 (the first day of spring) and September 23 (the first day of autumn), the length of daylight and dark periods is the same. These dates are called vernal and autumnal equinoxes, respectively. (The seasons are reversed in the Southern Hemisphere, with autumn in March, winter in June, spring in September, and summer in December.)

In this project, you will learn what solar radiation is and how its intensity can be determined. You will also investigate the difference of intensity of radiation at different angles and how this changing intensity creates seasons.

Getting Started

Purpose: To model the concentration of energy from the Sun.

Materials

transparent tape
ruler
flashlight

graph paper with ¼-inch (0.63-cm) or smaller grid
marking pen

Procedure

1. Tape the ruler along the side of the flashlight so that a 4-inch (10-cm) section of the ruler extends past the bulb end of the flashlight.

2. Lay the graph paper on a table.

3. Turn the flashlight on and hold it above the paper so that the ruler touches the edge of the paper and the flashlight shines down on the paper.

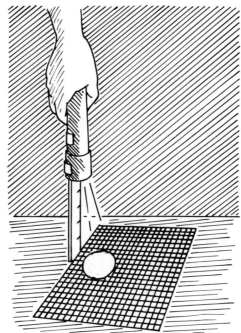

Figure 9.1

4. Draw around the bright center circle of light you see on the paper (see Figure 9.1).

5. Count all the squares that are at least halfway in the light. Figure 9.2 shows check marks in the counted squares.

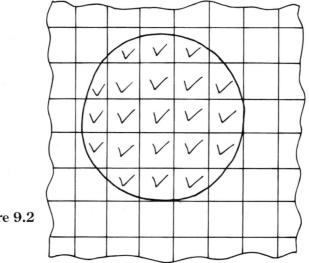

Figure 9.2

6. Calculate the estimated area covered by the light. Multiply the number of squares checked by the area of each square (area = length × width).

Example:

number of squares checked = 21

     area of each grid square = length × width

                       = 0.25 inch (0.63 cm) × 0.25 inch (0.63 cm)

                       = 0.0625 square inch (0.40 cm^2)

     area of the lighted circle   = estimated squares × area of each square

                       = 21 × 0.0625 square inch (0.40 cm^2)

                       = 1.31 square inches (8.4 cm^2)

Results

The lighted area depends on the light used and the size of the grid. In the example, the 21 lighted squares covered an area of 1.31 square inches (8.4 cm^2).

Why?

Radiation, such as light, is energy transferred by waves. **Solar radiation** (radiation given off by the Sun), like that from the flashlight, contains different kinds of radiation, including infrared radiation (heat) and visible light. Visible light is used in this investigation to indicate how concentrated all the radiation from the light source is. The radiation is most direct when the surface and the direction of the radiation are perpendicular to each other, demonstrated by shining the light perpendicular to the surface of the paper. When light rays strike the surface at an angle, the same amount of light must now be spread out over a larger area. Since a greater area must share this light, every point on the surface receives fewer rays, and thus less intense light.

The same thing happens with the Sun and Earth, producing our **seasons** (regularly recurring periods of the year characterized by a specific type of weather). When the Sun's rays strike an area of Earth more directly (as in summer), that area receives more intense light and heat from the Sun. However, when the Sun's rays strike that same area of Earth at a greater angle (as in winter), that area receives less intense light and heat from the Sun. In this investigation, the smaller the lighted area produced by the light rays, the more concentrated or intense the radiation.

Try New Approaches

How does the angle at which radiation strikes a surface affect the intensity of the radiation? Repeat the experiment three times, first holding the flashlight perpendicular to the paper. Then, without moving the end of the ruler touching the paper, tilt the flashlight about 45° from the paper. Finally, tilt the flashlight about 10° from the paper. Use a different color pen to trace the outline of each lighted area on the paper. Note that the amount of radiation leaving the flashlight is the same regardless of the angle of the flashlight. So the size of the lighted areas indicates how concentrated or intense the radiation from the flashlight is. **Science Fair Hint:** Display the overlapping circles, labeling each with its estimated area and the angle of light that produced it.

Design Your Own Experiment

1a. Design an experiment to measure the change in the intensity of solar radiation during the day. One way is to secure graph paper to a board so that it will lie flat. Place the board outdoors on a level surface in a sunny area. Bend a large paper clip to make a stand for a 2-inch (5-cm)–diameter Styrofoam ball. Stand the ball on the graph paper. Using the technique in "Try New Approaches," determine the area of the ball's shadow at different times during the day. *Note:* As the area of the light increases, its intensity decreases.

b. To determine the changes in intensity of solar radiation from season to season, repeat the previous experiment at noon on the first day of each week for as many weeks as possible.

2. Design an experiment to relate light intensity to the angle of the Sun's rays. One way is to record the angle of the Sun's rays each time the light intensity is measured. Determine these angles by hammering a large nail, such as a 16d nail into a block of wood until it stands straight and strong. Set the block outdoors, using a carpenter's level to ensure that the block is level. Tape a string to the top of the nail. Ask a helper to stretch the string from the nail to the end of its shadow. Use a protractor to measure the angle between the nail and the string, as shown in Figure 9.3. This is the angle of the shadow. Determine the angle of the Sun's rays using this formula:

$$\text{angle of Sun's rays} = 90° - \text{angle of shadow}$$

For example, in Figure 9.3 the angle of the shadow is 50°, so the angle of the Sun's rays is:

$$\text{angle of Sun's rays} = 90° - 50°$$
$$= 40°$$

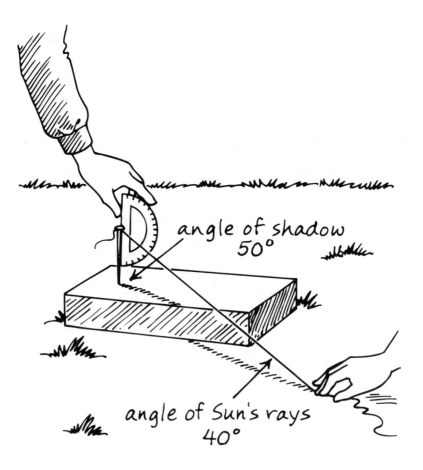

angle of shadow
50°

angle of Sun's rays
40°

Figure 9.3

Get the Facts

Solstice is combined from two Latin words, *sol* (Sun) and *stare* (to stand). Solstices are the times when the Sun, in its apparent annual motion, is at its greatest angular distance north or south of the *celestial equator,* which is an imaginary line in the sky projected from Earth's equator. On the days of the solstice, in summer and winter, the periods of daylight or darkness are the longest of the year. How does the position of the Sun affect the angle of the Sun's rays? Where is the Sun at the equinoxes? How do these positions affect the angle of its rays? For information, see Richard Moeschl, *Exploring the Sky* (Chicago: Chicago Review Press, 1993), pp. 12–15.

PART IV

The Planets

10 Solar System Scale: Miniature Model

Our solar system consists basically of the Sun, the nine planets (celestial bodies that orbit a sun), and their moons, asteroids, comets, and space debris. The boundary of the solar system is called the heliopause, which is the limit the solar winds reach. *Solar winds* are streams of charges escaping from the Sun's atmosphere and flowing into the solar system. From the heliopause, the solar system is about 18.6 billion miles (29.8 billion km) across. The Sun is the largest celestial body in the solar system, having a diameter of about 870,000 miles (1,392,000 km). Pluto is the smallest planet at about 1,434 miles (2,294 km) across. All of the millions of asteroids and comets are much smaller than Pluto.

In this project, you will make a 3-D model to represent the sizes of celestial bodies in the solar system. You will also learn how to represent the distances between planets and between planets and their moons.

Getting Started

Purpose: To build a 3-D scale model of Earth.

Materials

drawing compass

metric ruler

sheet of colored poster board

scissors

index card

pen

Procedure

1. The diameter of Earth is about 7,973 miles (12,757 km). Using the metric scale of 1 cm = 3,000 km, calculate the diameter of the model Earth as follows:

Earth's actual diameter ÷ 3,000 km/cm = model Earth's diameter

12,757 km ÷ 3,000 km/cm = 4.252 cm

Rounding the number to the closest centimeter, the model Earth's diameter would be 4 cm.

2. Use the compass to draw two circles with diameters of 4 cm (radius 2 cm) on the poster board.

71

3. Cut out the circles, then cut along a straight line (radius) from the circumference to the center of each circle.

4. Fit the two circles together at a 90° angle to each other (see Figure 10.1)

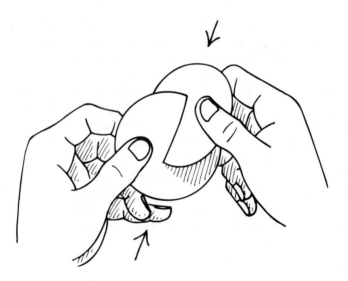

Figure 10.1

5. Prepare a legend showing the scale of the model by folding the index card in half. Write the scale, "1 cm = 3,000 km," on one side of the card. Stand the card alongside the model.

Results

You have made a scale model of Earth.

Why?

A **scale model** is a replica made in proportion to the object it represents. A **solar system** is a group of celestial bodies that orbits a star called a sun. **Planets** are large celestial bodies that orbit a sun. Models of bodies in our solar system, such as Earth, are valuable because they allow an observer to compare the relative sizes and distances of large things more easily.

Try New Approaches

How does the size of Earth compare with the other planets in the solar system? Make more scale models, using the diameters of the planets given in Appendix 3. **Science Fair Hint:** Attach threads to the models and suspend them from a 4-foot (1.2-m) or longer dowel. Support the ends of the dowel, then take a picture of the models. Use the photo and models in your science fair display.

Design Your Own Experiment

1. A **satellite** is a celestial body or man-made body that revolves about another celestial body. Earth has one natural satellite, the Moon. Design a scale model that accurately represents the size of both Earth and the Moon and the average distance between them. The Moon's diameter is 2,173 miles (3,476 km). The average distance between the centers of Earth and the Moon is about 240,250 miles (384,400 km). Use the scale 1 cm = 3,000 km. Make one sphere to scale for Earth and another for the Moon. Label the models "Earth" and "Moon." Calculate the length of string needed to represent the distance between them. Measure and cut string of the necessary length. Tape one end of the string to the center of the model Moon and the other end to the center of the model Earth. Ask helpers to hold the models, stretching the string taut between the models, while you take a photo (see Figure 10.2). Display the photo along with a legend indicating the actual sizes and distances along with the scale you used.

Figure 10.2

2. The planet Jupiter has many moons. Its four largest are collectively called the **Galilean satellites** because they were discovered in 1610 by Galileo (1564–1642). Make a model of Jupiter and the Galilean called Ganymede. The diameter of this moon is 3,293 miles (5,268 km). It orbits 668,750 miles (1,070,000 km) from Jupiter. Jupiter's diameter is 89,875 miles (143,800 km).

3a. The average distance between Earth and the Sun is about 93 million miles (149 million km). This distance is called an **astronomical unit** (AU) and is used as a measure of distance in the solar system. The AU measurement for any planet can be calculated by dividing the planet's distance in miles (km) by 93 million miles (149 million km). For example, Mercury is about 36 million miles (58 million km) from the Sun, thus the AU distance between the Sun and Mercury is:

36,000,000 miles ÷ 93,000,000 miles = 0.387 AU

58,000,000 km ÷ 149,000,000 million km = 0.389 AU

Rounding the answer to the nearest tenth, Mercury is 0.4 AU from the Sun.

Prepare a data table like Table 10.1, giving the average distances of the planets in miles (km) from the Sun (distances shown are from Appendix 3) and in AU units. Calculate the AU distance to the nearest tenth as in the preceding example.

Table 10.1 Planets' Average Distances from the Sun		
Planet	Average Distance, millions of miles (millions of km)	Distance, AU
Mercury	36 (58)	0.4
Venus	68 (108)	
Earth	93 (149)	1.0
Mars	143 (228)	
Jupiter	486 (778)	
Saturn	892 (1,427)	
Uranus	1,794 (2,870)	
Neptune	2,810 (4,497)	
Pluto	3,688 (5,900)	

b. Use the AU distances to draw a scale model of the solar system.

Get the Facts

1. By definition, natural satellites (moons) are smaller than the planets they orbit. Even the smallest known planet in our solar system, Pluto, has a satellite called Charion. Pluto is smaller than Earth's moon, and Charion is even smaller. Find out more about the natural satellites of the planets. Do all the planets have satellites? How do their sizes compare with the size of the planets they orbit? Make models of the planets and their satellites. For information, see Patrick Moore and Will Tirion, *Guide to Stars and Planets* (Cambridge: Cambridge University Press, 1993).

2. The sixth planet from the sun, Saturn, is known for particles that orbit the planet, creating what looks like rings as observed from Earth. Make a model of Saturn. How many rings are there? What are they made of? How large are they? What causes them to change in visibility? For information, see Ann-Jeanette Campbell, *New York Public Library Amazing Space* (New York: Wiley, 1997), pp. 124–128.

11 | Barycenter: The Balancing Point

Our solar system consists of the Sun and the many millions of celestial bodies, including large planets and microscopic dust particles, which orbit around it. As a unit, the solar system has a center of mass, its balancing point. At this point, the system would balance like a spinning plate atop a circus performer's balancing stick. This point, called the barycenter, is the exact point about which all the bodies in the solar system orbit. Since the Sun is vastly larger and heavier than all the other bodies combined, the solar system's barycenter is very close to the Sun—but not at the Sun's center. Thus, while all the other solar system bodies seem to orbit the Sun, they, including the Sun, are actually orbiting a point in space just beyond the Sun's outer layer.

Binary bodies are two celestial bodies held together by mutual gravitational attraction. In this project, you will learn how mass affects the location of their barycenter. You will discover the mathematical relationship between the masses of binary bodies and their distances from their barycenter. You will prepare a model of the Earth-Moon system and determine the orbit that each body follows as it orbits the barycenter of the system. You will also discover the location of the barycenter for most planet-moon systems.

Getting Started

Purpose: To model the barycenter of binary bodies.

Materials
one-hole paper punch
½-by-3-inch (1.25-by-7.5-cm) piece of thick paper, such as a file folder
6-foot (1.8-m) or longer cord
1 pound (454 g) modeling clay
food scale
5⁄16-by-48-inch (0.78-by-120-cm) wooden dowel
yardstick (meterstick)

77

Procedure

1. Use the paper punch to make a hole in each end of the piece of paper.
2. Bend the paper to bring the holes together. Thread one end of the cord through the holes. Tie a knot to hold the holes together. You have made a paper sling for the dowel.
3. Tie the other end of the cord to a ceiling hook or other supporting object. Adjust the length of the cord so that the paper sling hangs about chest high.
4. Using the food scale, measure two 8-ounce (227-g) pieces. Shape each piece into a ball.
5. Stick one end of the dowel into one of the clay balls to a depth equal to the radius of the ball.
6. Slide the free end of the dowel through the paper sling.
7. Repeat step 5 using the remaining clay ball on the other end of the dowel.
8. Determine the balancing point by moving the dowel back and forth in the sling until it balances (see Figure 11.1).

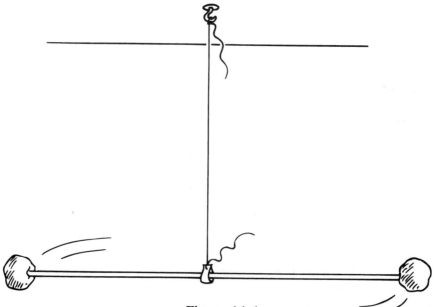

Figure 11.1

9. Measure and compare the distance between the center of each clay ball and the center of the paper sling.

10. Gently push one of the balls so that the dowel turns. Observe the motion of the clay balls.

Results

The balancing point is in the center of the dowel, an equal distance from each of the clay balls. The balls move in a circular path around the sling.

Why?

Binary bodies are two celestial bodies held together by mutual gravitational attraction. **Gravity** is a force of attraction between all objects in the universe. Examples of binary bodies are two stars, a planet and its sun, or a planet and its moon. Binary bodies behave somewhat as if they were connected by a dowel. Their center of gravity is called the **barycenter** (the point between two binary bodies where their mass seems to be concentrated and the point about which they rotate). If the masses of the binary bodies are equal, the barycenter lies at an equal distance from each body. Binary bodies **revolve** (move in a circular path about a point) about their barycenter.

Try New Approaches

Different masses affect the distance of each body from the barycenter. Mold the clay into one large ball and one tiny ball. Weigh the balls on the food scale and prepare a Celestial Body Mass vs. Distance table like Table 11.1. Call the mass of the smaller ball m_1. Let the mass of the larger body equal m_2. Call their distances from the center of each clay ball to the barycenter d_1 and d_2, respectively. Use the dowel and sling to find the barycenter as in the original experiment (see Figure 11.2). Measure d_1 and d_2.

Table 11.1 Celestial Body Mass vs. Distance		
Celestial Body	**Mass**	**Distance from Barycenter, inches (cm)**
1	$m_1 = ?$	$d_1 = ?$
2	$m_2 = ?$	$d_2 = ?$

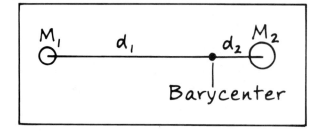

Figure 11.2

For example, when m_1 =1 ounce (28 g) and m_2 =15 ounces (426 g), and d_1 = 45 inches (112.5 cm), then d_2 = 3 inches (7.5 cm). Notice that mass and density have an inverse relationship, which means that when one term increases, the other decreases.

In our example, $m_1 \times d_1 = m_2 \times d_2$, or $m_1/m_2 = d_2/d_1$ = 3/45, which reduces to 1/15. Thus, m_1 lies 15 times farther from the barycenter than does m_2, and m_2 is 15 times more massive than m_1.

Design Your Own Experiment

The Earth and Moon are binary bodies with a barycenter that lies about 1,000 miles (1,600 km) beneath Earth's surface on the side facing the Moon. Design a model to show the paths of Earth and the Moon as they orbit their barycenter. One way is to use a 2-by-12-inch (5-by-30-cm) strip of poster board. In the center of one end of the strip make a dot and draw a circle with a 4-mm radius around the dot. Label this circle "Earth." Lay a ruler across the length of the poster board and make two dots at these distances from the center of the circle: 3 mm and 240 mm. Label the first dot "Barycenter." Draw a second circle as small as you can around the second dot. Label this circle "Moon." Stick a pushpin through the barycenter dot into a pencil eraser on the underside of the dot (see Figure 11.3). Holding the pencil in one hand, rotate the strip around the pushpin in a counterclockwise direction. Use the equation in the previous experiment and these distances to calculate the ratio of the Earth/Moon masses. Compare this ratio with a ratio of Earth's and the Moon's mass found in a reference book. Display the model and a legend of the scale.

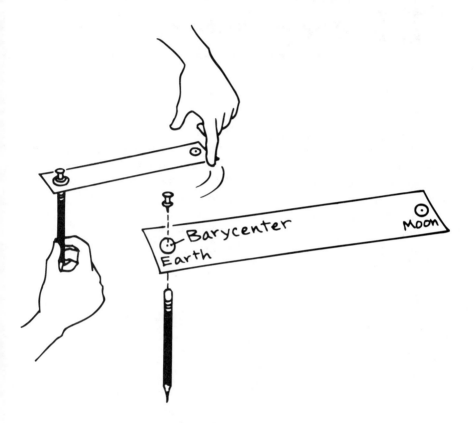

Figure 11.3

Get the Facts

The average barycenter of our solar system lies just outside the surface of the Sun. It changes depending on the location of the planets. Jupiter, the most massive planet, has the greatest effect. Find out more about the barycenter of binary bodies in the solar system. Where does the barycenter lie for most planet-satellite (moon) systems? Which planet has such a massive moon that the barycenter lies in the space between them? For information, see Thomas R. Watters, *Planets: A Smithsonian Guide* (New York: Macmillan, 1995).

12

Orbital Eccentricty: How Circular a Celestial Body's Path Is

Planets are large celestial bodies that orbit a sun. In our solar system, the nine known planets are Mercury, Venus, Earth, Mars, Jupiter, Saturn, Uranus, Neptune, and Pluto. The seventeenth-century German astronomer Johannes Kepler (1571–1630) discovered that planets follow an elliptical path. A planet's orbital eccentricity is how much the orbit deviates from being a circle.

In this project, you will discover the basic shape of planetary orbits as stated in Kepler's first law of planetary motion. You will also determine how nearly circular orbits are and make models.

Getting Started

Purpose: To draw the planets' orbital shape as described by Kepler.

Materials

pencil

ruler

12-inch (30-cm)–square piece of white poster board

12-inch (30-cm)–square piece of thick cardboard

2 pushpins

10-inch (25-cm) piece of string

Procedure

1. Draw a straight line across the center of the poster board.

2. Near the center of the line, draw two dots 4 inches (10 cm) apart.

3. Place the poster board on the cardboard. Stick one pushpin in each of the dots on the line.

4. Double the string and tie a knot as close to the free ends as possible.

5. Position the loop of string around the pushpins.

6. Place the pencil point against the inside of the loop.

7. Keeping the string taut, guide the pencil around the inside of the string to draw a closed curved on the paper (see Figure 12.1). Keep the paper and loop of string for the next experiment.

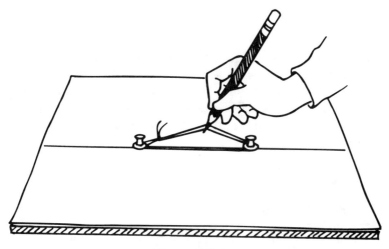

Figure 12.1

Results

You have drawn a closed curve with a longer, major axis (greatest distance across) and a shorter, minor axis (least distance across), as shown in Figure 12.2.

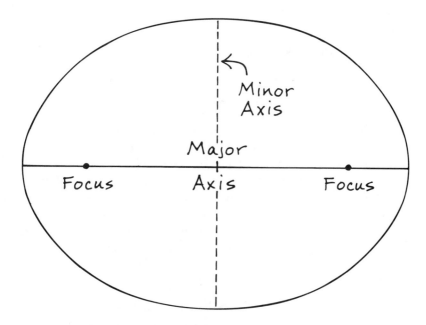

Figure 12.2

Why?

The closed curve in this investigation is an oblong figure called an ellipse. An ellipse is the figure drawn around two fixed points called the **foci** (the singular is **focus**). The distance from one focus to any point on the ellipse and back to the other focus is equal to the length of the major axis. In 1609, Kepler published his **first law of planetary motion,** which states that the orbits of the planets around the Sun are ellipses in which the Sun is at one focus.

Try New Approaches

1. How does the distance between the foci affect the shape of the orbit? Draw four circles with the pushpins these distances apart: 0 inches (0 cm), 3 inches (7.5 cm), 5 inches (12.5 cm), and the length of the loop of string.

2. **Eccentricity** is a ratio that describes how much an ellipse deviates from the shape of a perfect circle. To calculate eccentricity, divide the distance between the foci by the length of the major axis. Calculate the eccentricity of each of the orbits you have drawn. Use the results to formulate statements comparing the eccentricity values of different ellipses. For example, as the eccentricity increases, the shape is more or less circular/elliptical/linear.

Design Your Own Experiment

1a. Aphelion is the point in a planet's orbit farthest from the Sun. Perihelion is the orbital point closest to the Sun. Design an investigation to use the distance of a planet at aphelion and at perihelion to determine an orbit's eccentricity. One way is to fold a sheet of white copy paper in half, long sides together. Open the paper and stick two pushpins on the fold line at a distance apart less than the length of a loop of string. Place the loop around the pushpins and draw an ellipse as before. Draw a sun at one focus and two small circles of equal size on the ellipse, one at each end of the major axis (see Figure 12.3). The circles represent a planet at perihelion and aphelion. Measure the perihelion distance (a) and aphelion distance (b) on your drawing. Use your measurements and the following example to determine the eccentricity of the planet.

$$a = \text{distance at aphelion}$$
$$b = \text{distance at perihelion}$$

$$a - b = \text{distance between foci}$$
$$a + b = \text{length of major axis}$$
$$e = \text{eccentricity}$$
$$e = (a - b) \div (a + b)$$
$$= ?$$

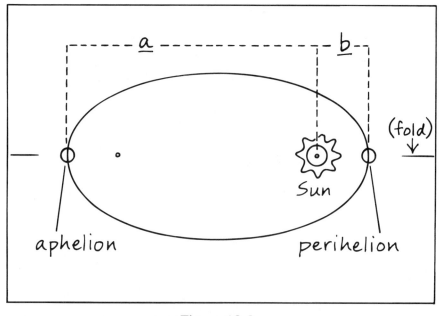

Figure 12.3

b. Calculate the eccentricity of each of the nine planets using their perihelion and aphelion distances in Appendix 3. Display your work in a table that includes columns for the following data on each planet: distance at aphelion and at perihelion, distance between foci, length of major axis, and eccentricity.

2. Make scale drawings of the orbits of Mercury, Venus, Earth, and Mars. Let 1 cm equal 10 million km (1.0×10^7). To determine where to place the pushpins, you need to determine the focal difference using the perihelion and the aphelion, and the length of the major axis. The length of the string will be twice the sum of the aphelion plus the perihelion, plus about 4 cm to tie the knot in the string. Prepare a measurement table similar to Table 12.1, then use the table to make your drawings.

Example:

$$\text{Earth's aphelion} = (1.52 \times 10^8 \text{ km}) \div (1.0 \times 10^7 \text{ km/cm})$$
$$= 15.2 \text{ cm}$$
$$\text{Earth's perihelion} = (1.47 \times 10^8 \text{ km}), (1.0 \times 10^7 \text{ km/cm})$$
$$= 14.7 \text{ cm}$$
$$\text{distance between foci} = \text{aphelion} - \text{perihelion}$$
$$= 15.2 \text{ cm} - 14.7 \text{ cm}$$
$$= 0.5 \text{ cm}$$
$$\text{length of string} = 2 \times (\text{aphelion} + \text{perihelion}) + 4 \text{ cm}$$
$$= 2 \times (15.2 \text{ cm} + 14.7 \text{ cm}) + 4 \text{ cm}$$
$$= 63.8 \text{ cm}$$

Table 12.1 Scale of Orbital Distances				
Planet	Aphelion, cm	Perihelion, cm	Distance between Foci, cm	String length, cm
Earth	15.2	14.7	0.5	63.8

Get the Facts

Johannes Kepler was an excellent mathematician who used other scientists' observations to develop a theory of planetary motion. On whose work did Kepler rely? How long did he work to arrive at his explanations? How did Kepler's model compare with the models of earlier astronomers, such as Aristotle, Ptolemy, and Copernicus? For information, see David Filkin, *Stephen Hawking's Universe* (New York: Basic Books, 1997), pp. 33–38.

13 Planetary Phenomena: Planetary Movement Relative to Earth

Ancient astronomers saw the planets as wandering stars. Later astronomers learned that the planets orbit the Sun in a plane nearly the same as the Sun's equator. That's why planets appear to follow the same path as the Sun across our sky.

In this project, you will model the movement of Venus and determine where in its orbit it appears highest above our horizon when viewed from Earth, which is the best viewing position. You will also use a model to measure the angular separation of Venus and the Sun and see how this distance changes from one night to the next.

Getting Started

Purpose: To model the position of Venus in relation to Earth.

Materials

2 coins (quarter and nickel)
10-inch (25-cm)–square piece
    of white poster board
pencil
ruler

drawing compass
transparent tape
10-inch (25-cm) piece of string
protractor

Procedure

1. Place the quarter in the center of the poster board. Trace around the quarter, remove the coin, and label the circle "Sun."

2. Make a dot in the center of the circle. Label the right edge of the poster board "West" and the left edge "East."

3. From the center dot, draw a 3-inch (7.5-cm) line toward the bottom edge of the poster board.

4. Measuring from the center dot, mark a second dot at 2 inches (5 cm) and a third dot at the end of the line.

5. Center the nickel over the dot at the end of the line. Draw around the nickel, remove the coin, and label the circle "Earth."

6. With the compass, draw two circles around the Sun. Draw one circle with a 2-inch (5-cm) radius and a second with a 3-inch (7.5-cm) radius. The smaller circle represents Venus's orbit, and the larger circle Earth's orbit.

7. Mark eight X's on Venus's orbit and number them as shown in Figure 13.1. Each X represents a position of Venus in its orbit around the Sun.

8. The line from the Sun to Earth passes through Venus's position 1X. Using the ruler and pencil, draw a dashed line from the center of the Earth circle to each of the other X's as shown.

9. Tape one end of the string to the center of the Earth circle.

10. Lay the protractor on the diagram so that the center point of the protractor is on the center of the Earth circle as shown. Holding the end of the string, stretch the string so that it lies across the protractor and passes through 2X on Venus's orbit. Read the Sun-Earth-Venus angle and record it in a Venus Elongation Data table like Table 13.1.

11. Repeat step 10 for each of Venus's positions (X's) on the circle representing Venus's orbit.

Table 13.1 Venus Elongation Data	
Venus's position (Xs)	Elongation
1X	
8X	

Results

When Venus moves to positions 1X and 5X, the string passes through the Sun, and Earth, the Sun, and Venus align with one other. In positions 2X, 3X, 4X, 6X, 7X, and 8X, an angle forms between them. The largest angle forms at positions 2X and 8X.

Why?

Venus, like other planets, is visible from Earth because the Sun's light reflects off it. Venus and Mercury are the two **inferior planets** (planets closer to the Sun than is Earth). The angular separation between the Sun and a planet as viewed from Earth is called **elongation.** When Venus

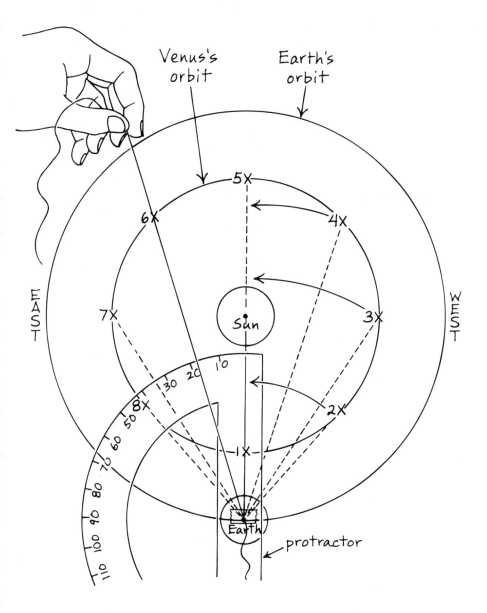

Figure 13.1

(and Mercury) rises before the Sun in the early morning, it is seen west of the Sun and is said to be at western elongation—as in positions 2X, 3X, and 4X. When it sets after the Sun in the early evening, it is seen east of the Sun and is at eastern elongation—positions 6X, 7X, and 8X.

As seen from Earth, the four most significant positions of the inferior planets are positions 1X, 2X, 5X, and 8X. Position 1X and 5X show the Sun and Venus in conjunction. **Conjunction** is the position of celestial bodies when they are on the same celestial longitude line as viewed from Earth. Inferior planets can be in conjunction twice in one revolution, at inferior conjunction and at superior conjunction. Position 1X is called an **inferior conjunction.** This is where an inferior planet lies between Earth and the Sun, but Venus does not **transit** (when an inferior planet passes across the Sun's disc) the Sun. Position 5X is called a **superior conjunction.** This is where a planet lies on the opposite side of the Sun from the Earth, but is not in **occulation** (the passing of a celestial body across a celestial longitude line between another celestial body on the same line). In other words, at inferior and superior conjunction, Venus is either above or below the Sun, but the planet is not visible because it is lost in the Sun's glare. The elongation at both the inferior and superior conjunctions is 0°.

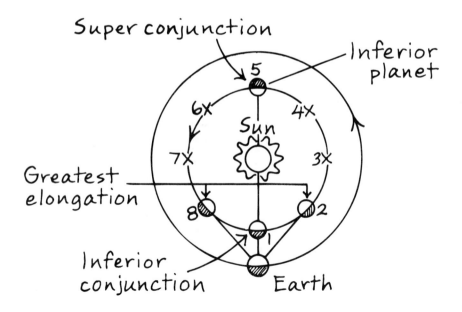

Figure 13.2

At positions 2X and 8X, Venus is at its maximum angular separation between the Sun and a planet as seen from Earth. Called **greatest elongation,** this is never more than 47° for Venus. For Mercury, being even closer to the Sun than Venus, greatest elongation never exceeds 28°. Greatest elongation is the best time for viewing the inferior planets because the Sun is lower below the horizon, making the sky darker (see Figure 13.2).

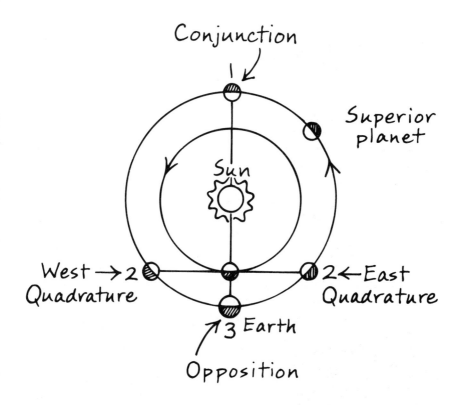

Figure 13.3

Try New Approaches

Model the positions of the **superior planets** (those farther from the Sun than is Earth). Repeat the experiment using a 4-inch (10-cm) line and circles with 3-inch (7.5-cm) and 4-inch (10-cm) radii. Place the superior planet on the outer circle. Find the following positions (see Figure 13.3):

1. elongation angle = 0° (when the Sun and the superior planet are in conjunction with the planet on the far side of the Sun from Earth)

2. east and west elongation angles = 90° (**east and west quadrature,** when the elongation angle is 90° toward the east or west)

3. elongation angle = 180° (**opposition,** when a superior planet is on the side of Earth opposite the Sun)

Science Fair Hint: Prepare diagrams of the inferior and superior planets with their positions labeled.

Design Your Own Experiment

As viewed from Earth, the inferior planets are never far from the Sun. The greater their elongation, the more visible they are. Because they are close to the Sun, they are visible only when the Sun is just a short distance below the horizon. At their eastern elongation, Mercury and Venus can be seen above the western horizon after the Sun sets. At their western elongation, they can be seen above the eastern horizon before the Sun rises. Venus has the greater elongation, so it is easier and safer to view than Mercury. Design an experiment to measure how the elongation of Venus changes from day to day. One way is after the Sun sets or just before it rises, to use your hands to estimate the planet's angular distance from the point on the horizon where the Sun sets or rises. To estimate angular distances, hold your hand at arm's length and make a fist. Each fist equals about 10° of angular separation. **CAUTION:** *Never look directly at the Sun. It can damage your eyes.* (See Chapter 3, "Altitude: Vertical Coordinate," for more information about hand measurements.)

Get the Facts

A planet's *sidereal period* is the time it takes the planet to complete one revolution around the Sun. For Venus, it is about 225 Earth days. What is a synodic period? How do the synodic and sidereal periods of a planet differ? For information, see the *National Audubon Society Field Guide to the Night Sky* (New York: Knopf, 1995), pp. 45–46.

14 Orbital Period: Time of Revolution

Kepler's third law of planetary motion was published approximately 10 years after his first two. This law expresses the relationship between the orbital period of a planet and its average distance from the Sun. An orbital period is the time it takes a planet to make one revolution, which is once around its orbit.

In this project, you will discover how mass and distance affect a celestial body's orbital period. You will model the effect of the barycenter on the period of a planet. You will also discover how Bode's law predicts the distances of planets.

Getting Started

Purpose: To determine the effect of distance on the orbital period of an orbiting planet.

Materials

$\frac{3}{8}$-inch (0.93-cm) metal washer
6-foot (1.8-m) cord
ruler
2 pairs of safety goggles
timer
helper

Procedure

Note: This activity is to be performed outdoors.

1. Tie the washer to the end of the cord.
2. On the cord, measure 18 inches (45 cm) from the washer and tie a knot in the cord.
3. Measure 18 inches (45 cm) from the knot and tie a second knot in the cord.
4. Repeat step 3, making a third knot.

5. Put on a pair of safety goggles. In an area away from other people, hold the cord at the first knot—18 inches (45 cm)—from the washer and swing your arm so that the washer spins above your head.

6. Find the slowest speed that will keep the washer "in orbit."

7. Ask your helper to wear safety goggles and be your timekeeper (see Figure 14.1). When your time keeper says, "Start," count the number of revolutions the washer makes. A **revolution** is one turn around a circular path.

Figure 14.1

8. Stop counting when the timekeeper says, "Stop," at the end of 10 seconds.

9. Calculate the **orbital period,** T, (time per revolution) of the washer by dividing the time by the number of revolutions. For example, if you counted five revolutions in 10 seconds, the orbital period would be:

   T = orbital period = time ÷ number of revolutions

                       = 10 seconds ÷ 5 revolutions

                       = 2 seconds/revolution

This is read as 2 seconds per revolution and means that it took 2 seconds for the washer to travel 1 revolution.

10. Repeat steps 5 to 9 four times for a total of five trial measurements.

11. Repeat steps 5 to 10 for the two other distances: 36 inches (90 cm) at the second knot, 54 inches (135 cm) at the third knot.

12. Record the data in an Orbital Period by Orbit Distance table like Table 14.1.

Table 14.1 Orbital Period by Orbit Distance						
Orbital Distance inches (cm)	Orbital Period (T), seconds/revolution					
	Trial 1	Trial 2	Trial 3	Trial 4	Trial 5	Average
18 (45)						
36 (90)						
54 (135)						

13. Make a bar graph of the average orbital periods. Place distance (the **independent variable** that you changed) on the horizontal axis. Place the orbital period (the **dependent variable** that changes in response to the independent variable) on the vertical axis.

Results

The longer the cord, the greater the orbital period.

Why?

Kepler's **third law of planetary motion** states that the more distant a planet's orbit from the Sun, the greater the planet's orbital period. This experiment shows that the law works for an object spinning in a circular path.

Try New Approaches

How does the mass of the orbiting object affect its orbital period? Repeat the experiment using two washers. As before, provide just enough energy to keep the washers in a circular orbit. In a physics book, find the formula for the orbital period in relation to mass. Do your experimental results agree with the formula?

Design Your Own Experiment

1. The farther the barycenter (center of mass) is of planet-Sun system from the Sun, the greater the orbital period of revolution of the planet. Use two dowels of different lengths to illustrate this principle. First, determine the center of mass of each dowel by balancing it on your finger. Where your supporting finger touches the rods is their center of mass. Mark the center of mass on each dowel. Rest one end of each dowel on a level surface, such as a floor or table, with a few inches (cm) between them. The flat surface represents the Sun. Hold the dowels up vertically, steadying them with the tips of your fingers. Lean both dowels forward the same amount so they will fall in the same direction. Release both at the same time. Which hits the surface first? For your display you may wish to make a drawing like Figure 14.2 showing the results of this experiment.

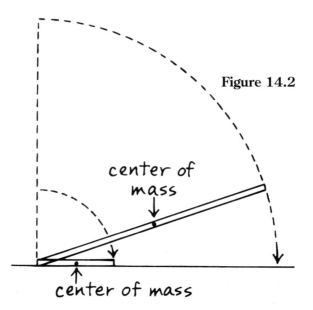

Figure 14.2

center of mass

center of mass

2a. Design an experiment to measure the orbital periods of one of the visible planets. Note that Mercury is too close to the Sun to be seen and the movements of Jupiter and Saturn are very slow. The visibility and relatively fast movements of Venus and Mars make them the best subjects. One experiment is to measure the average angular motion of the selected planet per day. Use this to calculate the orbital period, which is the time for 1 revolution of 360°. Starting on day 1, use a cross-staff (see Chapter 2 for instructions on making and using a cross-staff) to measure the angular separation between the planet and a star. Take five measurements on the first day and average them. Take five measurements 7 days later and average them. Record measurements in an Angular Separation Data table like Table 14.2. Calculate the orbital period of the planet using these steps:

- Calculate the difference (D_1) between the average angular separation on the first and seventh day.
- Calculate the time (t_1) for D_1, which is the time between the two sets of measurements. Thus, t_1, = 7 days.
- Calculate the portion of the revolution (D_2) the planet moved in 6 days by dividing D_1 by the degrees in 1 revolution, which is 360°. $D_2 = D_1/360°$
- Calculate the orbital period (T) using the following equation:

$$T = t_1/D_2$$

Table 14.2 Angular Separation Data					
Angular Separation, °					
	Trial 1	Trial 2	Trial 3	Trial 4	Trial 5	Average
D_1						
D_2						

b. Kepler's third law states that a planet's orbital period (time of one revolution around the Sun) depends on its average distance from the Sun. This equation is:

$$P^2 = k \times r^3$$

where P is the orbital period, r the average distance from the Sun, and k a constant. If P is in years and r is in AU, k equals 1. Using the known radius of the visible planets (see Appendix 3), calculate the orbital period of each. Note that the radius must be expressed in AU, which can be determined by taking the average distance of the planet from the Sun and dividing by the average distance of Earth from the Sun. For example, for Mercury the radius in AU can be determined using miles or km: 36 ÷ 93 = 0.39 AU.

c. Using the known orbital period and the experimentally determined orbital periods in the previous experiment, calculate your experimental percentage error. (See Appendix 2 for information about percentage error.) What is retrograde motion and how would it affect your percentage error? For information about retrograde motion, see Dinah Moche, Astronomy (New York: Wiley, 2000), pp. 197–200.

Get the Facts

The German astronomer Johann Titius (1729–1796) showed that the distances of planets from the Sun follow a fixed formula when measured in astronomical units. The formula is known as *Bode's law*. What is this pattern? Why isn't it called Titius's law? What significant role did the pattern play in the discovery of the asteroids and some of the planets? How accurate are the distances using the formula? For information, see Nancy Hathaway, *The Friendly Guide to the Universe* (New York: Penguin, 1994), pp. 190–192.

15 | Spheroids: Bulging Bodies

At one time, people believed Earth to be flat. The Greek philosopher and mathematician Pythagoras (c. 580–c. 500 B.C.) may have been the first known person to propose that Earth is a sphere. People scoffed at the idea until 350 B.C., when Aristotle stated six reasons to believe it. Space travel and more accurate instruments have shown that Earth is not a true sphere but an oblate spheroid. It is flatter at the poles than at the equator.

In this project, you will discover how rotation affects the polar and equatorial diameters of Earth and other celestial bodies. You will determine the effect that period of rotation (time to make one turn), density (mass per volume), speed of rotation, and gravity have on the shape of rotating bodies.

Getting Started

Purpose: To determine why Earth's polar and equatorial diameters differ.

Materials

ruler
pencil
scissors
sheet of white copy paper
felt-tip pen
transparent tape
one-hole paper punch
¼-by-12-inch (0.63-by-30-cm) dowel
fine-point marker
helper

Procedure

1. Measure and cut two 1-by-7-inch (2.5-by-17.5-cm) strips from the paper.

2. On each strip, use the pen to mark dots in the middle of the strip at these distances from one end: ½ inch (1.2 cm); 3½ inches (8.75 cm); and 6½ inches (16.25 cm).

3. Use the pen to label the dots on one strip "B," "C," and "A." Label the dots on the other strip "A," "D," and "B."

4. Lay the strips end to end, then overlap the A dots. Tape the ends together (see Figure 15.1).

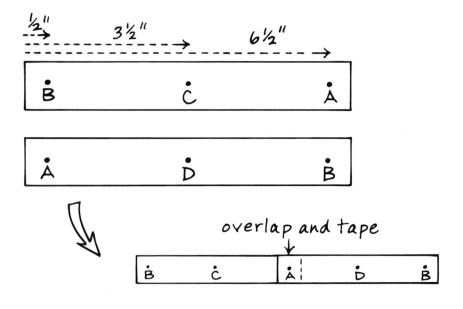

Figure 15.1

5. Bend the strips into a loop. Overlap the B dots and tape the ends together.

6. Punch holes through dots A and B. Enlarge the holes slightly so that the dowel can slide through them easily.

7. Push the dowel in through hole B, then out through hole A (see Figure 15.2).

8. Adjust the loop to form a true circular shape with hole A about 1 inch (2.5 cm) from one end of the dowel. Tape the loop to the dowel at A.

9. Use the marker to mark the point where hole B touches the dowel.

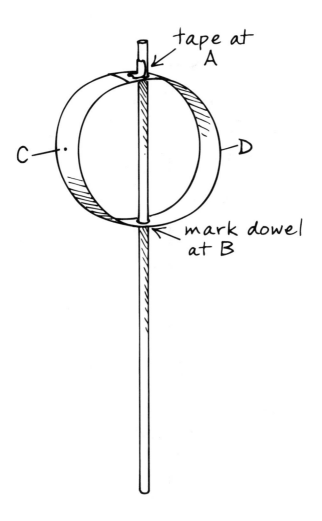

Figure 15.2

10. Measure the distance between points A and B and between points C and D. Record these distances as D_1 in column 2 of a Polar/Equatorial Diameter Data table like Table 15.1.

11. Hold the dowel between your palms below hole B and move your hands back and forth as fast as you can (see Figure 15.3). As the dowel turns, ask a helper to stop the motion by catching the dowel beneath hole B.

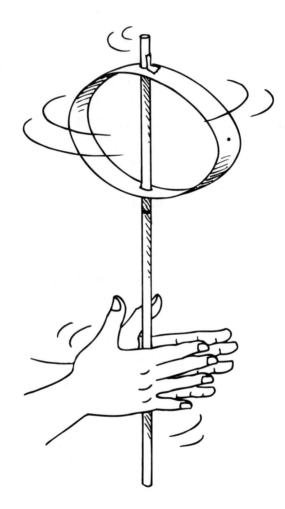

Figure 15.3

12. While your helper holds the dowel, repeat step 10, recording the distance as D_2 in column 3 of the data table.

13. Determine the change in the diameter created by the rotation using this equation:

$$\Delta D = D_2 - D_1$$

The sign of the difference in diameter merely indicates whether the change is an increase (+) or a decrease (–). Record ΔD in column 4 of the data table.

Table 15.1 Polar/Equatorial Diameter Data			
Location	Diameter, inches (cm)		
	D_1 (no motion)	D_2 (rotation)	ΔD
Polar (A to B)			
Equatorial (C to D)			

Results

While the loop is spinning, point B rises. The polar diameter between points A and B decreases. The equatorial diameter between points C and D increases.

Why?

Centrifugal force causes an object turning around a center to move outward from the center. This force causes point B to rise toward point A. The original shape of the loop was spherical. As it turned, it flattened at the poles (points A and B) and bulged at the equator (points C and D), becoming an **oblate spheroid.**

Like the paper circle, Earth spins around an axis (an imaginary north-to-south line through the center of a celestial body about which the body rotates) between its North and South Poles. Centrifugal force causes Earth to flatten at the poles and bulge at the equator. Thus, Earth's equatorial diameter exceeds its polar diameter. Astronomers refer to the difference between the equatorial and polar diameters as the **oblateness** (also called **ellipticity**) of the planet. The greater the difference between the diameters, the more oblate the planet. Thus, oblateness is the flattening of a spherical body, which is usually caused by rotation.

Try New Approaches

1. A planet's **period of rotation** is the time it takes to turn on its axis once. How does the period of rotation affect oblateness? Using your model, repeat steps 11 to 13, moving your hands slowly. Use the results and the period of rotations in Appendix 3 to explain why Earth has minor oblateness, while Mercury and Venus have little to no oblateness.

2. How does **density** (mass per unit volume) affect oblateness of a rotating body? Repeat the original experiment, using heavy card stock to make the paper strip. This increases the mass, which increases its density. Use the results and the densities in Appendix 3 to explain why the **Jovian planets** (Jupiter and other giant planets that are similar to Jupiter, namely, Saturn, Uranus, and Neptune) are more oblate than **terrestrial planets** (Earth and other planets that are similar to Earth, namely, Mercury, Venus, and Mars). **Science Fair Hint:** Ask a helper to take photographs of you performing each of the experiments. Use the pictures in your display.

Design Your Own Experiment

1. Compare the oblateness of the Sun, Earth's moon, and the planets in our solar system. Make a chart showing the oblateness of each. Oblateness is expressed as a percentage difference. Calculate oblateness by finding the difference between the equatorial diameter and the polar diameter. Divide this difference by the equatorial diameter. For example, Earth's equatorial diameter is 7,909 miles (12,756 km), and its polar diameter is 7,882 miles (12,713 km). Earth's oblateness is determined as follows:

oblateness = 7,909 miles (12,756 km) – 7,882 miles (12,713 km) ÷ 7,909 miles (12,756 km)
= 0.0034

2a. The rotation of Earth causes the **atmosphere** (blanket of gases surrounding a celestial body) to be thicker at the equator and thinner at the poles. How does the thickness of the atmosphere affect the appearance of stars? On clear moonless nights, compare the differences by viewing stars through thick and thin atmospheric layers. Note that an observer looks through more atmosphere when looking at celestial objects near the horizon than overhead. So, view a star near the horizon, then later the same night, at its highest altitude.

b. When you are away from home, observe the stars at different latitudes. Also compare viewing at sea level with viewing at a higher altitude, such as on a mountain. The closer you are to the polar and equatorial regions, the greater the differences you will see.

Get the Facts

At its equator, the Sun rotates at 4,500 miles (7,245 km) per hour. Earth's equator rotates at 1,035 miles (1,670 km) per hour. With a slower speed of rotation, why does Earth have a greater oblateness than the Sun? How does gravity affect oblateness? For information, see Isaac Asimov, *Guide to Earth and Space* (New York: Fawcett Crest, 1991), pp. 76–78.

16 Rotation: The Spinning of Celestial Bodies

Rotating celestial bodies spin around an axis, an imaginary line running through their centers. In 1851, French physicist Jean-Bernard-Léon Foucault (1819–1868) interpreted the motion of a pendulum as proof that Earth rotates on its axis. A pin at the end of his pendulum made marks in sand on the floor of the Panthéon in Paris. As the minutes passed, the direction of the pendulum remained the same, but the marks underneath it changed. This proved that the floor moved beneath the pendulum as a result of Earth's rotation.

In this project, you will determine how a pendulum moves at the North and South Poles. You will determine if the length of a Foucault pendulum affects the results. You will also learn how the apparent shift in the path of a pendulum varies at different locations on Earth.

Getting Started

Purpose: To model the motion of a pendulum at the North Pole.

Materials

marker
sheet of white copy paper
masking tape
10-inch (25-cm) string
metal washer
clothes hanger

Procedure

1. Draw a large star on the paper.

2. Tape the paper to a wall.

3. Tie one end of the string to the washer.

4. Tie the free end of the string to the center of the hanger.

5. Holding the hanger so that one end of it faces the star, lift the washer in the direction opposite the star on the paper. Release the string and let it swing toward and away from the star (see Figure 16.1).

6. While the washer is swinging, slowly rotate the hanger about one-fourth of a turn in a counterclockwise direction. Observe the direction that the swinging string moves in relation to the hanger.

7. Rotate the hanger another one-fourth of a turn in a counterclockwise direction and again observe the direction that the swinging string moves in relation to the hanger.

8. Repeat step 7 two times, bringing the hanger back to its original position.

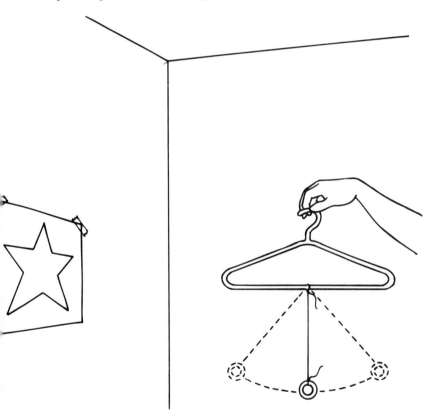

Figure 16.1

Results

The string continues to swing toward and away from the star. In relation to the hanger, the pendulum appears to move in a clockwise direction.

Why?

This investigation represents the motion of a **pendulum** (a weight that is suspended from a point and is free to swing back and forth) placed at the North Pole. The imaginary north-to-south line through the center of a body and about which it rotates is called an axis. The ends of the axis of a celestial body are called **poles.** The north and south end of an axis are called the North Pole and South Pole, respectively. The clothes hanger represents Earth rotating (turning on its axis). As viewed from above the North Pole, Earth rotates in a counterclockwise direction, like the turning hanger. When set in motion, the washer-and-string pendulum swings in one direction because of **inertia** (the tendency of an object at rest to remain at rest or of an object in motion to continue moving in a straight line unless acted on by an opposing outside force). In relation to the star, the swinging pendulum did not change direction, but in relation to the hanger, the pendulum seemed to move in a clockwise direction. This is because the hanger rotated in a counterclockwise direction. Thus, the pendulum's apparent motion was opposite to the rotation of the hanger.

Try New Approaches

How would the apparent path of a pendulum appear at the South Pole? Repeat the experiment, rotating the hanger in a clockwise direction. **Science Fair Hint:** Display photographs with labels indicating clockwise and counterclockwise rotations to represent the pendulum's swing at the poles.

Design Your Own Experiment

1a. Foucault's pendulum was a 220-foot (67-m) wire holding a 62-pound (28-kg) sphere. Find out if a shorter, lighter pendulum would work as well. Suspend a wire from a tree limb. To reduce friction and rotation, use two pieces of wire, one short, the other long. Tie both wires to a fishing swivel. Attach the short section of the wire to the limb and the longer section to a weight, such as a heavy bucket. Place a piece of poster board with a line drawn across it beneath the weight (see Figure 16.2). Set the pendulum in motion in the direction of the line. Observe the motion of the pendulum in relation to the line on the poster board.

Figure 16.2

b. Determine if the length of the wire affects the outcome. Use varied lengths of wire with the same weight.

c. Find out if the weight makes a difference. Keep the lengths of wire the same, but attach heavier or lighter objects.

Get the Facts

The path traced by Foucault's pendulum in Paris, at latitude 48°N, appeared to shift more than 10° per hour. (*Latitude* is angular distance in degrees north and south of the equator.) The degree of shift depends on latitude. Find out why. Learn how to calculate the shift for any given latitude. For information, see *Janice VanCleave's A+ Projects in Earth Science* (New York: Wiley, 1999), pp. 27–28.

Phases of Venus: Changes in Shape and Size

Galileo observed that, like the Moon, Venus had phases. His sightings led Galileo to question the established idea that everything in the universe orbited Earth. The cycle of phases of Venus noted by Galileo did not fit the pre-Copernican idea that all celestial bodies orbit Earth. However, they did fit with Copernicus's idea that Earth, Venus, and the other planets orbited the Sun.

In this project, you will model the phases of Venus as a morning and evening star. You will determine the position of Venus along its orbit by observing its phases. You will find its elongation, diameter, magnitude, and illumination. You will also learn about the planet's reflective surface.

Getting Started

Purpose: To model the phases of Venus, the morning star.

Materials
lamp
pencil
4-inch (10-cm) Styrofoam ball

Procedure

1. Set the lamp on a table and remove its shade.

2. Insert the point of the pencil into the Styrofoam ball.

3. Darken the room.

4. Holding the pencil, position the ball in front of but below the bulb of the lamp.

5. At a slight angle, slowly move the ball counterclockwise halfway around the light, stopping when the ball is behind and above the bulb of the light (see Figure 17.1). As the ball moves, note changes in the shape of its lighted side.

111

Figure 17.1

Results

In front of and behind the lamp, the lighted side of the ball is not visible. As the ball moves, the lighted part increases in size and shape.

Why?

Venus's path about the Sun is inclined only about 3°, but due to the planet's distance from the Sun, it generally is above or below the Sun's disk at inferior and superior conjunction. The angle of Venus's orbit is exaggerated in this experiment. In this investigation, the ball represents Venus, the light is the Sun, and you are an observer on Earth. When Venus is at inferior conjunction, between the Sun and Earth, it cannot be seen. The illuminated side of the planet faces away from Earth. Also in this position, the Sun's glare prevents the planet from being seen. As Venus moves, more of its illuminated side faces Earth. The apparent form of the sunlit surface of Venus is called a **phase.** During the phases of growing illumination, Venus is said to be **waxing.** When the planet is almost fully sunlit, it disappears due to the brightness of the Sun's light. It then moves beyond the Sun. In this position, when the Sun lies between Venus and Earth, Venus is at superior conjunction. At conjunction, the Sun and Venus are on the same longitude lines but are not in a straight line as seen from Earth.

During its counterclockwise movement from inferior to superior conjunction, Venus appears to the west of the Sun as viewed from Earth. When Venus's elongation is great enough, Venus rises before the Sun. At this time, it rises before the Sun in the eastern sky and shines so brightly that it is misnamed the "morning star." After the Sun rises, the sunlight is so bright that Venus is no longer visible.

Try New Approaches

How do the phases change during the second half of Venus's orbit around the Sun? Repeat the experiment, starting at superior conjunction and moving the ball to inferior conjunction. During this part of Venus's orbit, illumination decreases and Venus is said to be **waning.** It appears to the east of the Sun as viewed from Earth and follows the Sun across the ecliptic. At this time, Venus can be seen above the western horizon in the evening after the Sun has set. In this position, Venus is called the "evening star." **Science Fair Hint:** Use a diagram to show the positions of Venus when it is a morning and an evening star.

Design Your Own Experiment

1. Find a way to determine where Venus is in its orbit. Observe the phases of Venus to see whether Venus is waxing or waning. Binoculars that magnify 10× are powerful enough to see Venus's phases when it is close to Earth (a few days before and after inferior conjunction). At other times, you will need a telescope of at least 50×. For best results, use a 100× telescope with a dark blue or green filter to cut the Sun's glare. Diagram the position of Venus in relation to the Sun and Earth as shown in Figure 17.2. Note that the greatest elongation for Venus is about 47°. For information about viewing Venus, see Richard Moeschl, *Exploring the Sky* (Chicago: Chicago Review Press, 1993), p. 272. **CAUTION:** *Only make observations when the Sun is below the horizon. Never look directly at the Sun because it could permanently damage your eyes.*

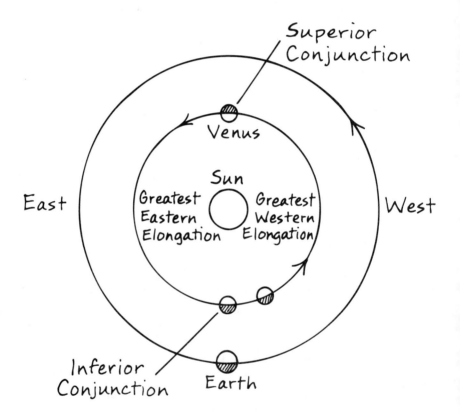

Figure 17.2

2. An **arc** is a segment of a circle, which measures 360°. Each degree can be further divided into 60 parts, called **minutes of arc,** and each minute of arc can be divided into 60 parts called **seconds of arc.** The

width of Venus's lighted part ranges from 10 to 61 seconds of arc in angular size. The angular size is 10 seconds of arc when Venus is near superior conjunction and 61 seconds of arc when approaching inferior conjunction. This information as well as the elongation, magnitude, and percentage of illumination of the planet appears in *Sky & Telescope* magazine each month and on the website www.galaxies.com. **Science Fair Hint:** Use this information, along with your diagrams and observations, to prepare a table for your display.

3. Try measuring the angular size of Venus using the techniques described in Chapters 1 and 2 of this book. **CAUTION:** *Only make observations when the Sun is below the horizon. Never look directly at the Sun because it could permanently damage your eyes.*

Get the Facts

Venus is bright partly because it is close to Earth. At its nearest, it lies about 100 times farther away than the Moon. But another reason is the reflectivity of its surface. *Albedo* is a measure of an object's reflective power. What makes Venus so reflective? What is its albedo and how does Venus's albedo compare to that of the Moon or Mercury? For information, see Patrick Moore, *Exploring the Night Sky with Binoculars* (New York: Cambridge University Press, 1986), p. 184.

PART V

Moons

Moon Phase: The Moon's Visible Lighted Surface

18

As seen from Earth, the apparent changes of the Moon's shape are called phases of the Moon. A complete cycle of the Moon's phases takes about 29½ days. The phases were observed but not understood by ancient astronomers.

In this project, you will determine what causes the different phases of the Moon. You will investigate the degree of change daily during a synodic month, the time between two successive new moons. You will also investigate the times of moonrise and moonset each day.

Getting Started

Purpose: To determine the cause of the phase of the Moon called the new moon.

Materials
walnut-size piece of modeling clay
pencil
flashlight

Procedure
1. Shape the clay into a ball and stick it on the point of the pencil. The clay ball is the model Moon.

2. In a darkened room, hold the flashlight at arm's length and shine the light toward your face.

3. Hold the model Moon midway between you and the light with the model aligned with the light bulb and slightly above it (see Figure 18.1).

4. Observe the surface of the clay ball.

Figure 18.1

Results

The light is very bright and the surface of the ball is difficult to see.

Why?

The Moon shines because it reflects light from the Sun. The side of the Moon facing the Sun is always sunlit. The side away from the Sun is always dark. As the Moon orbits Earth, an observer on Earth sees different portions of the Moon. The appearance of the illuminated surface of the Moon facing Earth is called a phase of the Moon. The Moon's orbit is at an angle of about 5° to the **ecliptic** (plane of Earth's orbit). Thus as seen from Earth, it usually appears to pass above or below the Sun's disk. When the Moon is in conjunction with the Sun, the side facing Earth is not illuminated. This phase is referred to as the **new moon.** The new moon rises with the Sun in the east and sets with the Sun in the west.

Try New Approaches

1. About 1 week after the new moon, the Moon has moved about one-quarter of the way around Earth. In this position, one-half of the side facing Earth is lit. Since this illuminated side is equal to about one-fourth of the Moon's total surface, this phase is called the **first quarter.** It is also called the first quarter because the Moon is one-quarter of the way through its lunar cycle. Demonstrate this phase by holding the model Moon to your left. Shine the flashlight directly at the model.

2. After about 2 weeks, the Moon is on the opposite side of Earth from the Sun. The side facing Earth is completely illuminated. This phase is called the **full moon.** Show a full moon by holding the model Moon behind you and shining the light directly on it.

3. The **third quarter** occurs around the beginning of the fourth week, which is three-fourths of the way through the lunar cycle. The illuminated quarter is opposite that of the first quarter. Show this by holding the model Moon in your right hand and shining the light from the left. **Science Fair Hint:** Diagram the positions of Earth, the Sun, and the Moon during the phases (see Figure 18.2). Add a Moon Data table showing the Moon's appearance at each phase.

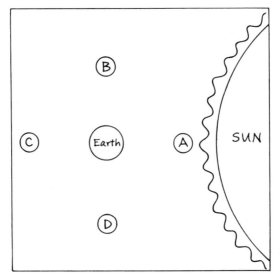

Figure 18.2

Design Your Own Experiment

1a. Determine the phase of the Moon each day during one **synodic month** (the time between two successive new moons). Draw a calendar with circles for the Moon's appearance in the squares. For each viewing, shade in the dark parts you see on the Moon. Use Table 18.1 to help you know when the Moon is visible. About 3 days before and after the new moon, the Moon is too close to the Sun to view safely. For these days, or when clouds obstruct your view, use the diagrams before and after these dates to **interpolate** (predict between data points) the times of moonrise and moonset. Color-code your calendar to distinguish actual observations from interpretations. **CAUTION:** *Never look directly at the Sun. It can damage your eyes.*

b. Make a table of the exact times of **moonrise** (when the moon appears to rise above the horizon) and **moonset** (when the moon appears to sink below the horizon) each day. You may find the information you need in the newspaper, hear it on television weather reports, or find it on the Internet.

Table 18.1 Approximate Times of Moonrise and Moonset		
Phase	**Moonrise**	**Moonset**
new moon	dawn	sunset
first quarter	noon	midnight
full moon	sunset	dawn
third quarter	midnight	noon

c. When the amount of illuminated surface is increasing, the Moon is said to be waxing. When decreasing, it is waning. Find out more about the waxing and waning phases and expand your observation chart. For information, see Dinah L. Moche, *Astronomy Today* (New York: Random House, 1995), p. 40.

Get the Facts

At times part of the Moon's surface is dimly illuminated by earthshine. What is earthshine? During what phase is earthshine most apparent? For information, see *Janice VanCleave's Solar Systems* (New York: Wiley, 1999), pp. 38–39.

19 Eclipses: Shadows of Earth and the Moon

A general definition of an eclipse is the blocking of one celestial body by another. A technical definition is the blocking of the light of one celestial body as it passes through the shadow of another body. A lunar eclipse occurs when Earth's shadow falls on and blocks the light of the Moon. A solar eclipse occurs when the Moon blocks the light of the Sun, so it fits the general definition of eclipse. But technically, what is called a solar eclipse is a special form of occulation, which is when a large celestial body passes in front of a smaller one.

In this project, you will model the positions of the Sun, Earth, and the Moon during solar and lunar eclipses. You will learn why eclipses do not occur every month, and you will determine the contact times when the stages of an eclipse begin and end. You will also identify the cause of partial and annular solar eclipses.

Getting Started

Purpose: To model a solar eclipse.

Materials
golf ball–size piece of modeling clay
2 pens
4-inch (10-cm) Styrofoam ball
flashlight

Procedure

1. Pull off a grape-size piece of clay and mold it into a ball.

2. Stick the clay ball on the pointed end of one of the pens. The clay ball represents the Moon.

3. Stick the point of the other pen into the Styrofoam ball. This ball represents Earth.

4. Use the remaining clay to stand the model Earth on a table.

5. In a darkened room, turn on the flashlight. Hold it in your left hand, about 12 inches (30 cm) from the Styrofoam Earth.

Figure 19.1

6. Hold the model Moon in your right hand, about 1 inch (2.5 cm) from the Styrofoam Earth. Move the clay Moon from the back side of the Earth toward the front in a counterclockwise direction (see Figure 19.1).

7. As the Moon moves, notice the shadow it casts on Earth's surface.

Results

The shadow of the clay Moon moves across the surface of the Styrofoam Earth.

Why?

Note: In astronomy the terms *occult* and *occultation* have nothing to do with astrology or anything supernatural. When the Moon passes directly between the Sun and Earth, it casts its shadow on a small part of Earth's surface. This is a model of a **solar eclipse,** which is when the Moon blocks the light of the Sun. To an observer in this shadowed area, the Sun seems to disappear for a few minutes. This event is called a **total solar eclipse.** Because Earth rotates, a small shadow of the Moon sweeps across Earth's surface. Because the shadow can be no larger than 170 miles (269 km) wide, only a few places on Earth experience a total eclipse at a given time.

Try New Approaches

1. When Earth's shadow falls on and blocks the light of the Moon, observers on Earth see a **lunar eclipse.** Continue the counter-clockwise rotation of the Moon around Earth. Notice that Earth casts its shadow across the entire Moon, not just a small part of it, as we saw in a solar eclipse.

2a. Most of the time during the new moon, the Moon's shadow does not fall on Earth's surface. This is because the Moon's orbit is at an angle of about 5° to the ecliptic. Model this by moving the Moon in front of Earth (on the same side of the flashlight) but slightly above or below the flashlight beam so that the Moon's shadow misses Earth.

b. To model a full moon when there is no lunar eclipse, repeat the previous experiment with the Moon behind Earth (on the opposite side of the flashlight), but just below (or above) Earth's shadow so Earth's shadow misses the Moon. **Science Fair Hint:** Draw a picture of the solar and lunar orbital paths as they appear from space. Show that only at or near the points where the two paths cross, called **nodes,** can an eclipse occur. Information about these paths can be found in astronomy textbooks.

Design Your Own Experiment

1a. All shadows have a penumbra (lighter outer area) and an umbra (darker inner part). During a lunar eclipse, observe and record contact time (when the Moon's edge either enters or leaves the penumbra or umbra of Earth's shadow). To check your results against predicted contact times, see Philip S. Harrington, *Eclipse: The What, Where, Why, and How Guide to Watching Solar and Lunar Eclipses* (New York: Wiley, 1997), pp. 18–23, 214–256. Another source is a current edition of the *National Audubon Society Field Guide to the Night Sky* (New York: Knopf, 1995), p. 685.

b. Because Earth's shadow is large, everyone on the dark side of Earth can see a lunar eclipse. But the Moon's shadow is small, so only a few people on Earth see a solar eclipse. If you are one of the lucky ones, find out the contact times for the solar eclipse. **CAUTION:** *Do not look at the Sun. It can permanently damage your eyes.* To safely view an image of the Sun during a solar eclipse, make a small hole in an index card. Let the light of the Sun pass through the hole onto a second card, the screen. Looking at the screen with your back to the Sun, change the distance between the two cards until the Sun's image focuses sharply on the screen. Mount the cards so that you do not have to hold them. Improve the view by shading the screen in a darkened area or inside a box. For more information about safely viewing a solar eclipse, see Harrington, *Eclipse,* pp. 24–36. For a safe way of using a telescope to study a solar eclipse, see *Janice Van-Cleave's Solar System* (New York: Wiley, 2000), pp. 14–15. For contact times for solar eclipses through the year 2017, pp. see Harrington, *Eclipse,* pp. 12–15, 121–214.

Get the Facts

The Sun is about 400 times larger than the Moon, and the Moon is about 400 times closer to Earth than the Sun is. This makes them appear from Earth to be about the same size, but not always exactly. During a total solar eclipse, the Moon appears to block the Sun from the view of observers on Earth. What happens if a solar eclipse occurs when the Moon is at or near apogee and Earth is at or near perihelion? In other words, what is an *annular eclipse*? What are the Sun-Earth-Moon positions during a partial *solar eclipse*? For information, see *VanCleave's Solar System,* pp. 20–23.

20 Craters, Maria, and Highlands: The Moon's Surface Features

The surface of Earth is ever changing, but the surface of the Moon looks much the same as it did when Galileo first pointed his telescope at it some 400 years ago. Why hasn't the Moon changed? The Moon has no atmosphere, so wind does not erode it. It has no rivers and it never rains, so moving water cannot scar the landscape. As a result, craters (large excavated areas created by meteor impact) formed millions of years ago remain unaltered today. Galileo saw smooth, dark areas that he named maria (singular, *mare*), meaning "seas." Today, we know that Galileo's maria are actually huge craters that long ago were filled with lava, which solidified.

In this project, you will make models of impact craters to see how object size affects crater size. You will learn how to map the surface of the Moon, and you will investigate the history of Moon mapping. You will also find out about the composition of maria and the surface's lighter areas, called highlands.

Getting Started

Purpose: To model the formation of a crater.

Materials

paper cereal bowl
plaster of paris
tap water
craft stick
2 or more sheets of newspaper
golf ball–size rock
petroleum jelly

Procedure

1. Fill the bowl with plaster of paris.

2. Gradually add water and stir with the craft stick until the mixture resembles a thick batter. The batter should hold its shape if you make a hole with the craft stick. *Note:* Discard the craft stick. Do not wash plaster down the drain. It can clog pipes.

3. Place the newspaper on the floor. Set the bowl in the center of the paper.

4. Cover the rock with a thick coating of petroleum jelly.

5. Standing and holding the rock chest-high above the center of the bowl, drop the rock (see Figure 20.1).

6. Carefully remove the rock from the plaster, disturbing the crater as little as possible.

7. Let the plaster sit until firm. Keep the bowl for display.

Results

The rock forces the plaster away from the point of impact. A ridge forms around the edge of the crater.

Why?

The Moon's surface is pitted with craters. A **crater** is a circular depression of any size. Large craters that are several miles (km) in diameter are called **basins.** Some of the smallest craters, at 10 to 20 **microns** (1 micron is equal to one-millionth of a meter) have been found etched on crystalline rocks brought from the Moon back to Earth by the *Apollo* astronauts. Most lunar craters are bowl-shaped **impact craters** caused by the impact of solid bodies. Both large and small craters are formed when meteorites slam into the Moon's surface. While in orbit about the Sun, these solids from celestial bodies are called **meteroids.** When a meteoroid strikes the surface of a celestial body it is called a **meteorite.** Because the Moon has no atmosphere, any object that hits it collides at full speed. In this investigation, you removed the rock so you could examine the impact crater. But on the Moon, the high-speed impact of larger meteorites produced an explosion upon impact. This explosion created an enormous amount of heat, which **vaporized** (changed to a gas) much of the meteorite and even some of the lunar material, leaving bowl-shaped craters. Small objects hitting with lesser force simply pushed the surface material aside, as was the case in this investigation. For small craters, if all the debris and crater walls were put back into the hole, they would fill it up.

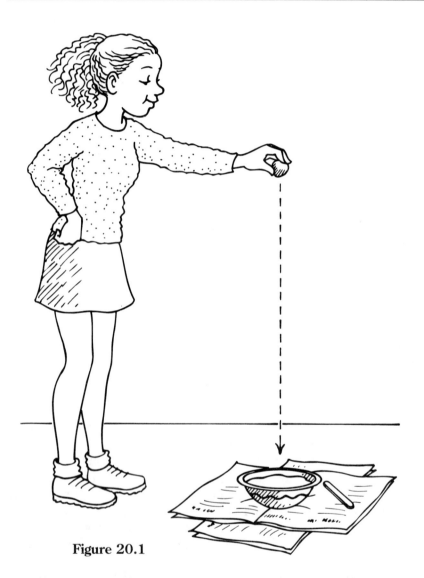

Figure 20.1

Try New Approaches

1. How does the size of the meteoroid affect the size of the crater? Investigate by using a larger, heavier rock. **Science Fair Hint:** Display two bowls with the crater models and the two rocks representing falling objects. For more information about Moon craters, see Heather Couper, *How the Universe Works* (Pleasantville, NY: Reader's Digest, 1994), pp. 48–51.

2. How does the speed of a meteoroid affect the size of the crater? Investigate by comparing the crater formed when a rock is dropped to one formed when the rock is thrown at greater speed. (Perform this experiment outdoors as there may be splattering of materials.)

3. What effect does the angle of impact have on craters? Repeat the original experiment, throwing the rock straight down, then at various angles. Compare the characteristics of the resulting craters. (Again, this experiment should be performed outdoors.)

Design Your Own Experiment

1a. The Moon has light and dark areas. The **maria,** or dark spots, on the Moon are the lowlands that cover about 20% of its surface. Maria have a lower elevation—by about 2 miles (3.2 km)—than the rest of the surface. The lighter areas, called **highlands,** are regions of higher than average elevation. The highlands are the older, cratered region of the Moon's surface. Highlands cover more than 70% of the surface. Find a way to map the Moon. Use binoculars or a telescope to study its surface. Make a scale drawing on graph paper of the features you see (see Figure 20.2). Provide a table like Table 20.1, identifying the features and their coordinates.

For the names of the Moon's features, see Richard Moeschl, *Exploring the Sky* (Chicago: Chicago Review Press, 1993), pp. 253–255. Another source is Dinah Moche, *Astronomy: A Self-Teaching Guide* (New York: Wiley, 1996), appendix.

Table 20.1 Moon Features		
Name of Feature	**East (E)/West (W)**	**North (N)/South (S)**
Copernicus (crater)	W26	N6
Mare Crisium (Sea of Crises)	E55	N16
Tycho (crater)	W13	S51

b. Watch the Moon for a month to determine which phase gives you the best view of the Moon's features. Draw maps of the different phases for comparison, including the **terminator** (the dividing line between the illuminated and unilluminated areas).

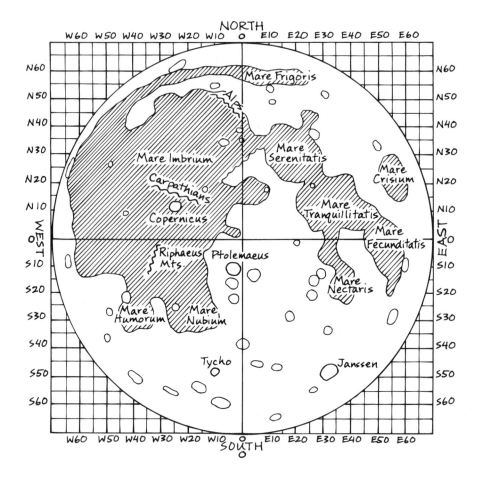

Figure 20.2

Get the Facts

1. The types of rocks that make up maria and highlands cause these surface features' different colors. What rock types make up these features? For information, see Moche, *Astronomy,* p. 264.

2. Galileo made the first sketches of the Moon in 1609. Find out how these scientists improved on Galileo's maps: Johannes Hevelius, John William Draper, G. B. Riccioli, and H. H. Schroeter. For information, see Moeschl, *Exploring the Sky,* p. 253.

21 | Galilean Satellites: Jupiter's Largest Moons

The four largest satellites of Jupiter are called Galilean satellites because they were discovered in 1610 by Galileo. Their names are Io, Europa, Ganymede, and Callisto, from closest to farthest from Jupiter.

In this project, you will discover the motion of each Galilean satellite during an Earth day (24 hours). You will plot the positions of the satellites as they move around Jupiter and determine their locations relative to Jupiter from a bird's-eye view above Jupiter's north pole, as well as from an observer's view from Earth. From actual observations, you will identify the Galilean satellites by name and learn more about each one.

Getting Started

Purpose: To determine the motion of Io during an Earth day (24 hours).

Materials
sheet of white copy paper
drawing compass
metric ruler
pencil
protractor

Procedure
1. The radius of Io's orbit is about 1.42×10^5 km. Using a scale of 6 mm = 1×10^5 km, calculate the radius of the orbit for a scale model as follows:

actual radius of Io's orbit/model radius of Io's orbit

1.42×10^5 km ÷ 1×10^5 km/6 mm = 25.2 mm

Rounding the number to the closest millimeter, the diameter of the scale model of Io would be 25 mm.

2. In the center of the paper, use the compass to draw a circle with a radius of 25 mm. The circle represents the orbit of Io.

3. In the center of the circle, make a small circle with a diameter of about 8 mm. This circle represents Jupiter.

4. Label the directions "East" and "West" on the paper as shown, in Figure 21.1 with "Facing South" at the bottom of the paper.

5. Make a dot on the east side of the circle. Number the dot 1. This dot represents the first observation location of Io.

6. To find the angular distance of Io's movement in one Earth day (24 hours), divide the angular distance of one revolution (360°) by Io's orbital period (1.77 days). Round the answer to the nearest whole number of degrees.

$$d = 360° \div 1.77 \text{ days} = 203°$$

7. Use the protractor to find a point on the circle 203° from the first dot. Make a dot on the circle at this point and number the dot 2.

8. Use the protractor to find a point on the circle 203° from dot 2. Make a dot on the circle at this point and number the dot 3. Repeat to find the location of dot 4.

9. Use the compass to draw 203° arcs as shown in Figure 21.1 to indicate the angular distance between the dots.

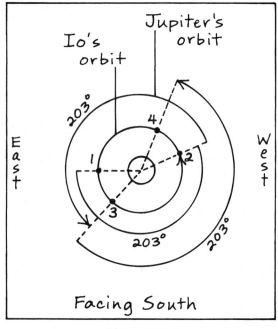

Figure 21.1

Results

The dots represent Io's position after 0, 1, 2, and 3 Earth days, with observation beginning at position 1.

Why?

A satellite is a celestial or man-made body revolving around another celestial body, such as the moon Io around Jupiter. Jupiter's four largest moons are called Galilean satellites. Io is the Galilean satellite closest to Jupiter. The orbital radius of Io is about 4.2×10^5 km (2.6×10^5 miles). In this project, you used a scale of 0.6 cm = 1×10^5 km. At this scale, the small center circle approximates Jupiter's diameter of 1.4×10^5 km (0.875×10^5 miles). The distance of 1 inch (2.5 cm) from the center of the circle approximates the orbital distance of Io from Jupiter's center.

The locations of dots 1, 2, 3, and 4 indicate the movement of Io over 3 Earth days (72 hours). During the first Earth day, Io moved counter-clockwise from dot 1 to dot 2, moving 203° around Jupiter. During the second Earth day, Io moved from dot 2 to dot 3, another 203°. Then during the third day, Io moved from dot 3 to dot 4, another 203°.

Try New Approaches

Assuming all of Jupiter's moons start at the same point on the first day of observation, how would their apparent distances from Jupiter appear at the end of 2 Earth days? Repeat the project using a data table like Table 21.1 to determine the angular distance each moon moves during 1 Earth day. Draw orbits at the correct radius from Jupiter's core using the same scale (0.6 cm = 1×10^5 km). Use different colored markers to represent each satellite. One at a time, plot the positions of each of the satellites for 2 days.

Table 21.1 Properties of the Galilean Satellites		
Name	Orbital Radius (km)	Orbital Period (days)
Io	4.2×10^5	1.77
Europa	6.7×10^5	3.55
Ganymede	10.7×10^5	7.15
Callisto	18.8×10^5	16.69

Design Your Own Experiment

1. The gravity (a force of attraction between all objects in the universe) of Jupiter has pulled the satellites into its equatorial plane, meaning the moons are basically in line with Jupiter's equator. At times the satellites with larger orbital radii appear closer than those with smaller radii. In the previous experiments, you modeled a face-on view of Jupiter's moons, but that's not how we see them from Earth. Find a way to model the edge-on locations of the moons as we do see them from Earth. Since we on Earth are almost perfectly aligned with the orbital planes of the moons, they seem to line up in a straight line across Jupiter's equator. One way to show this is to lay a sheet of clear plastic over the diagram of the positions of the satellites in the previous experiment. Make a red grape-size ball of modeling clay to represent Jupiter. Place this clay ball on the part of the plastic covering Jupiter. Using four different colors of clay, make four pea-size clay balls representing Jupiter's moons and place them on dot 1. Slip a piece of stiff cardboard or a book under the paper with the plastic on top, and raise the cardboard so the plane of the plastic is perpendicular to your face and Jupiter is directly in front of your eyes. Observe the positions of each of the satellites in relation to Jupiter. Two diagrams can be made as in Figure 21.2, one of the location of the satellites as seen from above Jupiter's north pole (above the plastic) and the other from the face-on view (as seen by an observer on Earth). Repeat this procedure, moving the satellites to their location after 1 Earth day and then again after 2 and 3 Earth days.

2. Observe Jupiter through a telescope for a period of 17 or more days. During this time, most of the satellites will have made many revolutions around Jupiter, but Callisto will have made only one. Design an experiment to plot the position of the satellites from day to day. Make four or more observations at least 1 hour apart to identify the satellites. They can be identified by the rate at which they move: from fastest to slowest, they are Io, Europa, Ganymede, and Callisto. For information on identifying the satellites on any specific day, see astronomy magazines, such as *Sky and Telescope* and *Astronomy,* for the month of the observation.

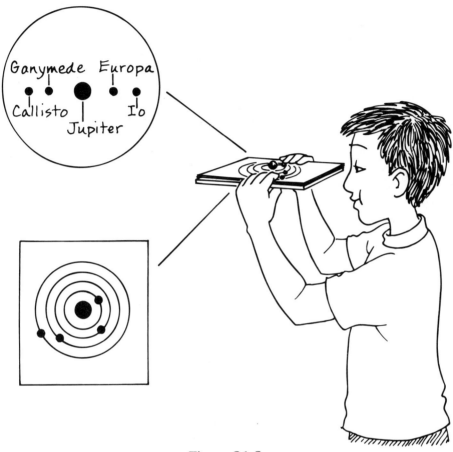

Figure 21.2

Get the Facts

At the time of the publication of this book, astronomers know of 16 satellites (moons) orbiting Jupiter. Others may be discovered as our instruments continue to improve. What are the names of these 16 moons? What are their orbital paths and periods? For information, see Brian Jones, *The Practical Astronomer* (New York: Simon & Schuster, 1990), p. 23.

PART VI

Stars

22 Celestial Sphere: Sky Globe

Stars look as if they are painted on a dome above Earth. To observers on Earth, this imaginary celestial sphere seems to move in a circle.

In this project, you will model the motions of Earth and the apparent motion of stars above Earth. You will also use the parts of a celestial sphere, such as its equator, lines of declination, and right ascension to determine the position of objects in the sky.

Getting Started

Purpose: To model the motion of the celestial sphere.

Materials

lemon-size piece of modeling clay
12-inch (30-cm)–square piece of white poster board
round toothpick
paper clip
narrow masking tape, ¼ inch (0.63 cm) wide, or cut to that width
2-quart (2-L) transparent bowl
8 to 10 stick-on stars

Procedure

1. Shape the clay into a ball. Flatten one side until the ball looks like half a ball. This is your model Earth.

2. Place the model Earth on the poster board, flat side down. Stick the toothpick through the center of the clay from top to bottom. Stick the paper clip in one side.

3. Run a strip of tape around the outside rim of the bowl. Turn the bowl upside down over the model Earth. Position the model Earth under the center of the bowl.

4. Stick a star on the bowl at the spot where the paper clip points. Number this star 1.

141

5. Rotate the bowl clockwise about one-eighth of a turn, and repeat step 4, numbering the star 2.

6. Repeat steps 4 and 5, placing six to eight more stars on the bowl and numbering them in order (see Figure 22.1).

Figure 22.1

Results

The stars form a circle above the model Earth.

Why?

Astronomers use the celestial sphere to locate celestial bodies such as stars, suns, moons, and planets. Earth lies at the center of this hollow ball, and stars appear to circle across the sky.

A model of the celestial sphere is called a **celestial globe.** The bowl in this experiment serves as one-half of a celestial globe. The clay ball represents half of Earth. The toothpick represents Earth's axis, the paper clip an observer on Earth. The **celestial equator** is an imaginary circle that divides the celestial sphere in half, is perpendicular to the sphere's axis, and is in line with Earth's equator. In this investigation, the celestial equator is represented by tape around the rim of the bowl.

The half of the celestial sphere above or north of the celestial equator is the **northern hemisphere.** The half of the celestial sphere below or south of the celestial equator is the **southern hemisphere.** (These regions of Earth are capitalized.)

To an observer on Earth (paper clip), the celestial sphere appears to rotate. The stars seem to move past the observer.

Try New Approaches

1. The celestial sphere is not a real object, nor does it rotate. Actually, it's Earth that does the rotating. If you could look down at Earth from above the North Pole, you would see Earth turn from west to east in a counterclockwise direction. Ask a helper to lift the bowl slightly while you rotate the model Earth, turning the paper counterclockwise. In what order do the stars move past the paper clip?

2. The imaginary axis of the celestial sphere aligns with Earth's axis. Thus, the north and south poles of the celestial sphere lie above the North and South Poles of Earth. Place a piece of masking tape at the north pole of your celestial globe and mark it with an X. Now place a stick-on star as near the X as you can, but not exactly on it. This represents Polaris, the star we call the North Star, which is within 1° of the celestial north pole. Where would you place the tape if this were a model of the southern hemisphere? **Science Fair Hint:** Display a photo of your model. Label the different parts of your celestial globe.

Design Your Own Experiment

1a. On Earth we create imaginary lines to help us locate places on Earth. These lines, called **longitude lines** (imaginary lines running around a celestial body or the celestial sphere from pole to pole that measure angular distances east and west of a designated 0° line) and latitude lines (running parallel to the equator), are seen on maps and globes. Using this idea, astronomers have created imaginary lines on the celestial globe to help them locate celestial bodies. **Hour circles** are **great circles** (circles around a sphere that have the same center point as the sphere), also called **celestial longitude lines** on a celestial globe that run from pole to pole perpendicular to the equator. These circles compare to Earth's lines of longitude. Design an experiment to show hour circles on your celestial globe, such as running thin strips of tape from rim to rim across the center of the outside of the bowl. Run another strip at a right angle to this strip, dividing the bowl into four equal parts.

b. Hour circles measure a celestial body's **right ascension,** or its east-west position. Right ascension is the celestial equivalent of longitude on Earth. It is measured in hours (^{h}), with 1 hour equaling 15°. More precisely, right ascension is the angular distance of a celestial body from the **vernal equinox** (position of the Sun on or about March 21 in the northern hemisphere when it crosses the celestial equator). Mark right ascension on your model. Place a dot on the celestial equator below one of the hour circles. Label the dot "0^h." Mark seven more dots evenly spaced along the celestial equator. Label the dots to the right of 0^h as 3^h, 6^h, 9^h, and so on to 21^h as in Figure 22.2.

c. **Declination** is the celestial equivalent to latitude on Earth. This angular distance is shown by imaginary lines circling the celestial sphere parallel to the celestial equator. A celestial body's declination is its angular distance in degrees north or south of the celestial equator. Mark a dot on the spot where the four hour circles cross the north pole (marked X). Label this dot "+90°." Mark the four hour circles where they cross the celestial equator at "0°." Mark two dots, evenly spaced, between 0° and +90° on each section of hour circle. Label the lower dots "+30°" and the upper ones "+60°." *Note:* In the northern hemisphere, the declinations are positive (+). In the southern hemisphere, they are negative (–).

d. Coordinates are two numbers that identify a location. Right ascension and declination make up a method of locating celestial bodies called the **equatorial coordinate system.** Demonstrate how to find the equatorial coordinates of stars. Stick stars on the bowl here and there. Tape the end of a 12-inch (30-cm) string at 90°, the North Pole. Pull the string down the side of the bowl so that it crosses one of the stars. Estimate the hours of its right ascension and the degrees of its declination. Star coordinates are written with the right ascension first. For example, the coordinates of the star in Figure 22.2 are 3^h, +30°. **Science Fair Hint:** Identify stars in your display by their equatorial coordinates. (See Fig. 22.2)

2. From where you live, can you see stars in both the northern and southern hemispheres? Observe the sky during as many different seasons as possible. Find coordinates and identify the stars. Make lists and maps of the stars in your region of the celestial sphere. For information about star identification, coordinates, and star maps, see Robin Kerrod, *The Star Guide* (New York: Macmillan, 1993).

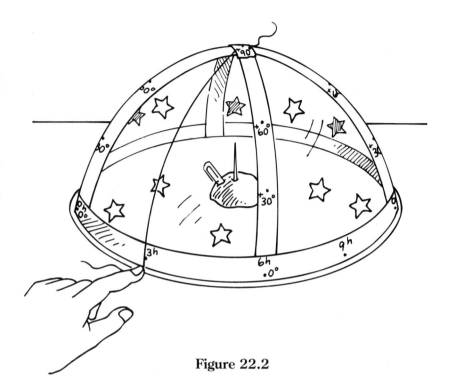

Figure 22.2

Get the Facts

1. The *horizontal coordinate system* uses the horizon as the reference circle. The zero point is north. *Altazimuth coordinates* are a combination of a celestial object's altitude (degrees above the horizon) and azimuth (degrees eastward around the horizon from north). For information, see David H. Levy, *Sky Watch* (San Francisco: The Nature Company, 1995), pp. 80–81.

2. To make an instrument to measure altazimuth coordinates, see *Janice VanCleave's Constellations for Every Kid* (New York: Wiley, 1997), pp. 156–160.

Zodiac Band: Background for the Ecliptic

23

From Earth, celestial bodies appear to move across the sky. This apparent motion is predictable from day to day. The position of each body can be described in relation to the zodiac, a belt of stars bordering the ecliptic, the Sun's apparent annual path.

In this project, you will use the zodiac to predict the location of the Sun and the naked-eye visible planets—Mercury, Venus, Mars, Jupiter, and Saturn—for any date. You will also learn how to predict whether Venus or Mercury will appear as a morning or evening "star."

Getting Started

Purpose: To demonstrate the position of the Sun during the year.

Materials

scissors
ruler
10-inch (25-cm)–square piece of white poster board
one-hole paper punch
drawing compass
protractor
pen
paper brad

Procedure

1. Cut a 1-by-7-inch (2.5-by-17.5-cm) strip from one edge of the poster board.

2. Punch a hole in the center and 2 inches (10 cm) from the end of the strip.

3. On the larger piece of the poster board, draw a circle 8 inches (20 cm) in diameter. Cut out the circle. This circle is your constellation wheel.

4. Use the protractor, ruler, and pen to divide the constellation wheel into twelve 30° pie-shape sections.

5. Around the edge of the wheel, write the names and dates of the 12 constellations from Table 23.1, one in each section, as shown in Figure 23.1.

Table 23.1 Zodiac/Solar Data		
Constellation	**Pronunciation**	**Date of Entry**
Pisces, the Fish	PYE-seez	Mar. 15
Aries, the Ram	AIR-eez	Apr. 16
Taurus, the Bull	TOR-us	May 15
Gemini, the Twins	JEH-muh-nye	June 16
Cancer, the Crab	KAN-sur	July 17
Leo, the Lion	LEE-oh	Aug. 17
Virgo, the Maiden	VUR-go	Sept. 17
Libra, the Scales	LEE-bruh	Oct. 18
Scorpius, the Scorpion	SKOR-pee-us	Nov. 17
Sagittarius, the Archer	sa-juh-TAIR-ee-us	Dec. 17
Capricornus, the Sea Goat	ka-prih-KOR-nus	Jan. 15
Aquarius, the Water Bearer	uh-KWAIR-ee-us	Feb. 13

6. Use the point of the compass to make a hole in the center of the wheel.

7. Place the hole of the strip over the hole in the wheel. Push the paper brad through the holes and secure.

8. Draw a sun design on the end of the strip even with the edge of the wheel. Write "Sun" by the design. On the strip, write "Earth" near the brad.

9. Hold the constellation wheel stationary while you rotate the strip so the Sun moves through the constellations in chronological (time) order. Note the following:

- The direction the Sun moves in relation to the constellations
- The position of the Sun in relation to the constellations
- The time interval between the constellations

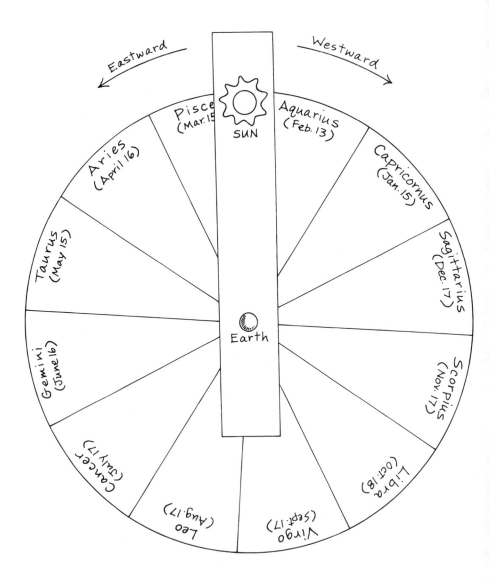

Figure 23.1

Results

The Sun appears to move counterclockwise and eastward in relation to the constellations. As it moves, it passes a different constellation about every 30 days.

Why?

If you could look down on the North Pole from space, you would see Earth revolving counterclockwise around the Sun. To observers on Earth, the Sun appears to move eastward among the stars along a path called the ecliptic. The ecliptic runs through a band of constellations that circle the celestial sphere. This band is called the **zodiac,** and the **constellations** (a group of stars forming a pattern) along the band are called **zodiac constellations.** In ancient times, skywatchers divided this band into 12 segments, each about 30° wide, with a constellation in each section.

As seen from Earth, the zodiac constellations provide a background for the Sun. At specified times, the Sun is said to be "in" a specific constellation. In this position, an imaginary straight line stretches from Earth through the Sun to the constellation.

When the Sun is in a constellation, its light is so bright that the stars in the constellation cannot be seen. The Sun and the constellation appear to move from east to west. From day to day, the Sun's apparent motion is about 4 minutes slower than that of the constellations. Thus, the constellations are about 1° farther west than the Sun each day. At the end of 30 days, the Sun is in the constellation 30° to the east. This makes the Sun appear to move eastward through the zodiac constellations.

Try New Approaches

Earth moves around the Sun; the Sun does not move around Earth. To show the relationship of Earth and the Sun to the zodiac constellations, cut a new strip of poster board 5 inches (7.5 cm) long. Punch and attach the constellation wheel as you did before. Label the brad "Sun." Draw the Earth at the short end of the strip. Draw a straight line from Earth through the Sun and past the brad to the other end of the strip. Draw an arrowhead that points to a constellation (see Figure 23.2). Rotate the strip as before, noting the constellation at the end of the arrow with each 30° movement of Earth. You might want to label the first strip you made "How It Seems to Be" and the second strip "How It Really Is."

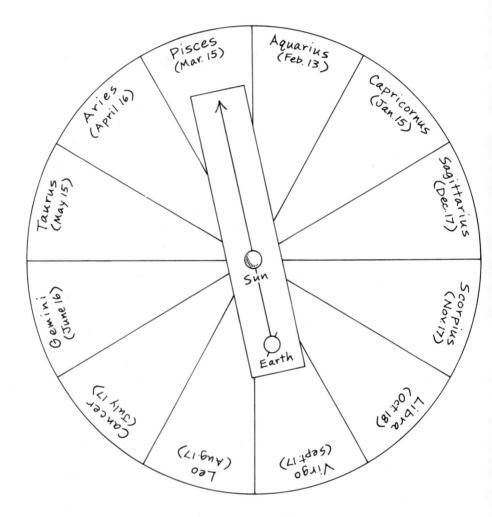

Figure 23.2

Design Your Own Experiment

1. As the planets appear to move across the sky, they follow paths very near the ecliptic, so the zodiac constellations also provide a backdrop for them. The planets visible with the naked eye are Mercury, Venus, Mars, Jupiter, and Saturn. When Venus and Mercury are west of the Sun, they are called morning stars. They rise before the Sun in the morning. When these planets are east of the Sun, they are called evening stars. They appear after the Sun sets in the evening. On the first and fifteenth of each month for 3 or more months, determine whether Venus is a morning or evening star. Do this by following these steps:

- Determine the Sun's position in a constellation for a specific date. For example, on January 15, 2003, the Sun enters the region of Capricornus. (The year affects the location of a planet on a certain day, but not the Sun.)

- Using a Planetary Longitudes table for the year in question, find the location of Venus and Mercury on that day. (For purposes of example, a portion of a planetary longitudes table is shown in Table 23.2.) On January 15, 2003, Venus is at longitude 248°. For planetary longitude tables for other years, see the *National Audubon Society Field Guide to the Night Sky* (New York: Knopf, use most current publication).

Table 23.2 Scale of Orbital Distances						
Year	Date	Mercury	Venus	Mars	Jupiter	Saturn
2003	Jan. 1	298	234	230	137	84
	15	287	248	239	138	83
	Feb. 1	287	266	250	133	83
	15	303	282	259	131	82

- On January 15, 2003, the Sun enters Capricornus, which is between 300° to 330° longitude. From the Constellation Longitudes chart shown in Figure 23.3, the longitude of the Sun entering Capricornus is 300°. Venus is at longitude 248° on January 15, 2003, and 248° is to the west of the Sun. So, on January 15, 2003, Venus will be a morning star.

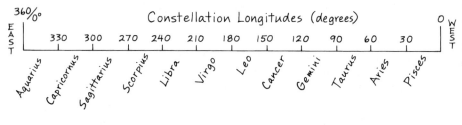

Figure 23.3

2. Use the procedure from the previous experiment to predict the locations of Mercury, Mars, Jupiter, and Saturn. Observe the sky to test your predictions.

Get the Facts

1. Most diagrams and descriptions of the zodiac show only 12 constellations, but the Sun actually passes through a thirteenth zodiac constellation each year. This constellation is called Ophiuchus. Where is Ophiuchus in relation to the other zodiac constellations? When does the Sun enter it? For information, see *Janice VanCleave's Constellations for Every Kid* (New York: Wiley, 1997), pp. 123–124.

2. You may have noticed that the dates associated with the constellations of the zodiac do not correspond with the dates in astrological horoscopes found in many daily newspapers. Why are these dates different? Why is astrology called a pseudoscience? For information, see *Janice VanCleave's Constellations,* pp. 102–105.

Circumpolar: Stars above the Horizon

Different stars are visible from different locations on Earth. Some appear every night and never set below the horizon. These are the circumpolar stars.

In this project, you will model the motion of circumpolar stars. You will determine which stars appear circumpolar to observers at different latitudes. You will find out how an observer's latitude affects the altitude of stars. You will also learn about northern and southern circumpolar stars that are easily seen.

Getting Started

Purpose: To model the motion of circumpolar stars at Earth's poles.

Materials

drawing compass

ruler

9-inch (22.5-cm)–square piece of poster board

9-inch (22.5-cm)–square piece of blue, transparent plastic (report folder works well)

black fine-point permanent marker or ballpoint pen

scissors

transparent tape

sheet of white copy paper

paper brad

Procedure

1. Draw a circle with a diameter of 3 inches (7.5 cm) in the center of the poster board.

2. Lay the sheet of blue plastic over the poster board. Use the marker to trace the circle onto it. Cut out the circle and discard it.

3. Lay the plastic over the poster board again. Line up the cutout with the circle. Tape the plastic and the poster board together at the top

edge. Cutting through both layers of the righthand side, remove a semicircle about 1 inch (2.5 cm) deep at its deepest point.

4. Using the compass, draw a circle 8 inches (20 cm) in diameter on the white copy paper. Cut out the circle.

5. Lift the plastic and center the paper circle on the poster board. With the compass point, punch a hole through the center of the poster board and the paper circle. Secure the paper circle and the poster board together with the brad.

6. Lower the plastic. Mark 20 to 25 dots in the exposed area of the paper circle, not too close to the outer edge (see Figure 24.1).

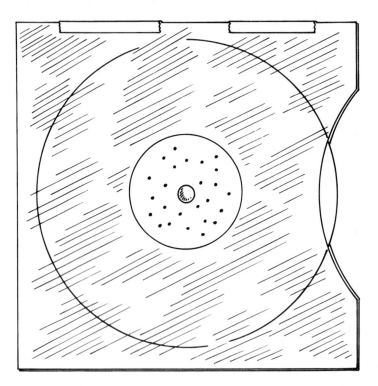

Figure 24.1

7. Turn the paper circle counterclockwise and observe the movement of the dots.

8. Turn the paper circle clockwise and observe the movement of the dots.

Results

The dots move, but remain within the opening of the sheet of plastic.

Why?

The brad represents a **celestial pole** (one of two ends of the axis of the celestial sphere). The dots in the opening represent the stars visible to an observer at latitude 90°N or 90°S, the North Pole or South Pole of Earth. (The stars seen at the two poles are different.) The blue edge represents the horizon, where the sky meets Earth. The **circumpolar stars** are always visible above the horizon from a given observation point on Earth.

From the North Pole, all visible stars are circumpolar. They appear to move counterclockwise around the north celestial pole. From the South Pole, all visible stars are circumpolar. They appear to move clockwise around the south celestial pole.

Try New Approaches

Model the motion of stars at lower latitudes. Lift the sheet of plastic from the model. Randomly add 40 or more dots to the outer region of the paper circle. Remove the brad and the paper circle. With the compass point, make a hole in the poster board about 1 inch (2.5 cm) below the existing hole. Center the paper circle on the new hole and secure with the paper brad, then lower the plastic (see Figure 24.2). Turn the paper circle counterclockwise and observe the movement of the dots. Turn the paper clockwise and observe again. Determine which stars are circumpolar. Also note how many of the stars that were circumpolar at latitude 90° are no longer circumpolar at the lower latitude represented by this experiment.

Design Your Own Experiment

Polaris, represented by the brad, is so near the north celestial pole (north end of the celestial sphere's axis) that it appears stationary to observers in Earth's Northern Hemisphere. Design an experiment to find out how the altitude of Polaris relates to the latitude of observers on Earth. Measure the altitude of Polaris at the latitude where you live and at other latitudes when you travel. Ask friends at different latitudes to make measurements for additional data. Record the data in a table. What conclusions can you draw from your data?

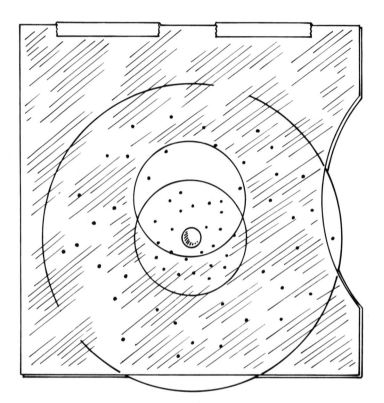

Figure 24.2

Get the Facts

Declination is the angular distance of a celestial body in degrees north or south of the celestial equator (0° declination). Declination on the celestial sphere aligns with the latitude lines of Earth. How can declination predict the visibility of a star at a given latitude? For information, see *Janice VanCleave's Constellations for Every Kid* (New York: Wiley, 1997), pp. 46–48.

25 Star Clock: Star Positions Indicate Time

From the Northern Hemisphere, Earth's rotation makes the stars appear to revolve counterclockwise around Polaris. Because the Big Dipper seems to move around Polaris, it can be used like the small hands of a clock to measure hours. This giant "sky clock" runs "backward," but its timekeeping is both accurate and predictable.

In this project, you will build a star clock that can be used to determine time on any clear night. You will observe the stars of the Big Dipper throughout the year and use your data to make a seasonal clock. You will also discover which of the Big Dipper's stars are circumpolar at your latitude, as well as the circumpolar stars at a corresponding latitude in the Southern Hemisphere. You will study the motion of four constellations near Polaris. A constellation is a group of stars forming a pattern. It also marks a specific part of the celestial sphere.

Getting Started

Purpose: To make a star clock that will use the position of the Big Dipper to tell time.

Materials

school glue
8-by-10-inch (20-by-40-cm) piece of white poster board
scissors
pushpin
paper brad

Procedure

1. Photocopy the Star Clock pattern pieces in Figure 25.1.

2. Glue the Star Clock pattern pieces to the poster board. After the glue has dried, cut out the pieces.

3. Assemble the two pieces by putting the circle with the stars on top of the circle with the months. The star circle will be called the star wheel.

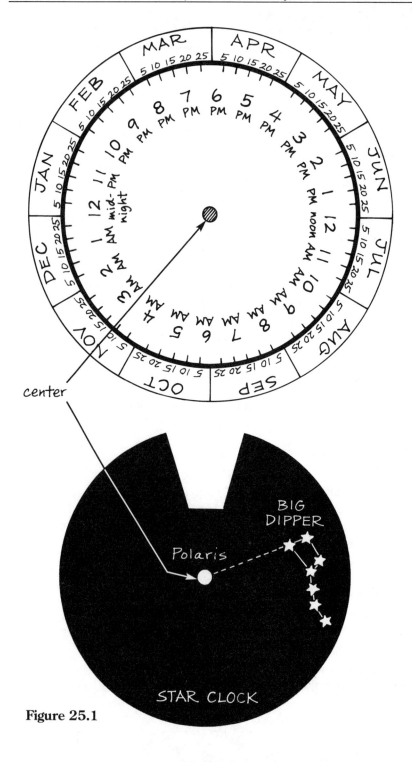

Figure 25.1

4. Use the pushpin to make a hole through the center of each circle, then insert the paper brad through the holes to hold the paper circles together.

5. Follow these steps to use the Star Clock:

- After dark, face north and locate the Big Dipper above the northern horizon.

- Hold the Star Clock so that the current month is at the top of the circle.

- Turn the star wheel until the outline of the Big Dipper lines up with the Big Dipper's position in the sky. Note that all of the Big Dipper stars are not circumpolar at every latitude.

- Time and dates appear in the cutout section of the star wheel. Using the date of the observation and the position of the Big Dipper, determine the time. How close is Star Clock time to actual clock time?

Results

Using the Star Clock and the location of the Big Dipper, you can tell the approximate time.

Why?

All the stars of the Big Dipper are circumpolar from latitudes of about 45°N and higher. Circumpolar stars always appear above the horizon and near a celestial pole. During a 24-hour period, the Big Dipper appears to revolve counterclockwise around Polaris. The daily circular path of the stars of the Big Dipper is called their **diurnal circle.** (*Diurnal* means "daily.") This apparent motion results from the revolution of Earth on its axis. Since this motion is predictable, you can use the position of the Big Dipper to estimate time.

Try New Approaches

In addition to the constellation (a group of stars forming a pattern and marking a specific part of the celestial sphere) Ursa Major (which includes the Big Dipper), three other constellations most visible near Polaris are Cassiopeia, Cepheus, and Ursa Minor (which includes the Little Dipper and Polaris). Use white correction fluid to draw these constellations on your Star Clock, using Figure 25.2 to determine where to position these stars in relation to one another. Use the Star Clock to locate the Big and Little Dippers and the four constellations at various times during the night.

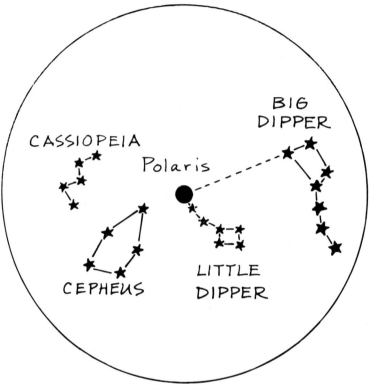

Figure 25.2

Design Your Own Experiment

1a. Earth makes one complete rotation on its axis in about 23 hours 56 minutes. Circumpolar stars appear to rotate in the same period. Because Earth also revolves around the Sun, stars do not appear exactly in the same place at the same time each day. They rise above the horizon 4 minutes earlier and move about 1° farther west in comparison to the night before. Your Star Clock can be used to indicate the motion of the stars of the Big Dipper from day to day. Check the accuracy of your Star Clock by observing the position of the Big Dipper's stars at the same time each night as often as possible during the year. *Note:* Compensate for daylight saving time when it is in effect.

b. Design a display chart to show the seasonal positions of constellations as they appear from where you live. Make a seasonal star calendar such as the one shown in Figure 25.3.

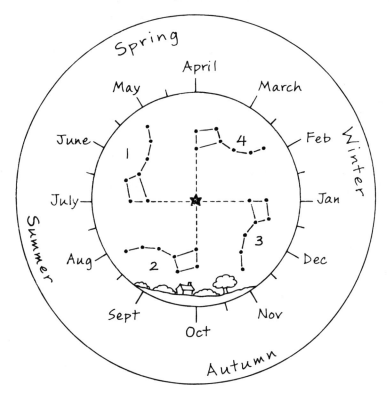

Figure 25.3

Get the Facts

1. The amount of the Big Dipper that is circumpolar at your latitude—
   in other words, always above the horizon—depends on your latitude. Find out your latitude from a map, then determine how many
   of the Big Dipper's stars are circumpolar. Do this by determining
   the range of declination of the stars for your latitude. For information, see pages 46–48 in *Janice VanCleave's Constellations for Every
   Kid* (New York: Wiley, 1997).

2. What other constellations or parts of constellations are circumpolar
   at your latitude? If you lived at the corresponding latitude in the
   Southern Hemisphere, which constellations would be circumpolar?
   For information, see Herbert S. Zim, *Stars: A Guide to the Constella-
   tions, Sun, Moon, Planets, and Other Feathers of the Heavens* (New
   York: Golden Press, 1985), pp. 98–99.

26 Star Systems: Multiple Stars

Most stars appear to be single stars. Telescopes have revealed, however, that more than half of all stars belong to double or multiple star systems in which stars appear to be close together.

In this project, you will model two types of double stars, optical and binary. You will learn how sky conditions affect observation of those doubles visible to the naked eye. You will also determine the orbital period of a pair of eclipsing binaries.

Getting Started

Purpose: To make a model of an optical double.

Materials

apple-size piece of modeling clay
$3/8$-by-36-inch (0.94-by-90-cm) dowel

Procedure

1. Divide the clay by pulling off a golf ball–size piece. Form both the large and small pieces into balls.

2. Lay the dowel on a table. Place the clay balls next to the dowel as shown in Figure 26.1.

3. Close one eye and look at the balls at eye level. Move your head right or left until the balls appear to lie side by side.

Results

The two clay balls appear close together.

Why?

Two stars that appear to be close together are called **double stars.** If the stars are actually far apart and have no true relationship to each other, they are called **optical double stars.** Like the clay balls in this experiment, optical doubles appear to be close because they lie along the observer's line of sight.

Figure 26.1

Try New Approaches

Binary stars are double stars that are relatively close to each other. Their mutual gravity binds them, and they revolve around a common point called the barycenter. To model binary stars, place a clay ball at each end of the dowel. (Note that distances between the stars are not being modeled, only their relationship.) Hang the dowel by a string so that it hangs level. Gently rotate the dowel about the supporting string (see Figure 26.2). The point where the string attaches to the dowel is the barycenter of this binary star system. To learn more, see Chapter 11, "Barycenter: The Balancing Point."

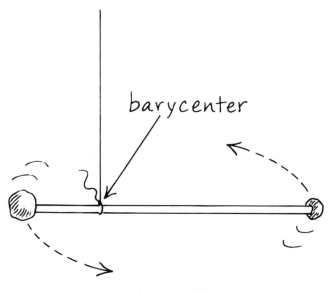

Figure 26.2

Design Your Own Experiment

1a. Investigate how sky conditions affect the identification of naked-eye doubles. Test your vision with the optical double stars Mizar and Alcor, which appear to be the second star from the end of the Big Dipper's handle (see Figure 26.3). Mizar is easy to see, but its double, Alcor, is much fainter. According to legend, before the invention of eyeglasses, Alcor was used by some cultures as a test of one's eyesight—only people with very good vision can see it with the naked eye. Look for Mizar and Alcor on different nights. Note the sky conditions, such as the phase of the Moon or the presence of clouds. How does the position of the pair in relation to the horizon affect your ability to see both stars?

b. Repeat the previous experiment using binoculars. ***Note:*** If you use a telescope, Mizar and Alcor look rather widely separated and you will discover that Mizar is itself a double star with a tiny, close companion star that is not visible with binoculars. Mizar is a binary star. For information about multiple star systems, see star charts in Terence Dickinson, *Nightwatch* (Buffalo, NY: Firefly Books, 1998), pp. 100–119.

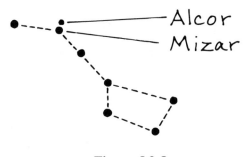

Figure 26.3

2. In an **eclipsing binary system,** our line of sight from Earth happens to align with the orbital plane of the two binary stars. As they periodically move in front of each other, the star in front partially or completely blocks the light of the star behind it, causing the total light from the star system to dim periodically. Algol is the name of the eclipsing binary system in the constellation Perseus. The two stars of the Algol system are Algol A and Algol B. Design an experiment to determine the changes in the **apparent magnitude** (how bright a celestial body appears as viewed with the naked eye from Earth) of Algol and the time cycle of these changes. To judge Algol's magnitude, compare it to Mirfak, the brightest star in Perseus. *Note:* If Algol is not visible, observe the eclipsing binary system Beta Lyrae in the constellation Lyra. For information, see Fred Schaaf, *40 Nights to Knowing the Sky* (New York: Henry Holt, 1998), pp. 110–113; and *Janice VanCleave's Constellations for Every Kid* (New York: Wiley, 1997), pp. 193–200.

Get the Facts

1. The period of rotation of binary stars can range from less than an hour to thousands of years. What binary star system has the shortest known orbital period? Why is the longest orbital period difficult to determine? For information, see Brian Jones, *The Practical Astronomer* (New York: Fireside, 1990), p. 46.

2. Stars in some binary systems are so close that they appear to be single stars even when viewed through a telescope. How do astronomers know there is a second star? For information, see spectroscopic binaries in Jones, *Practical Astronomer,* pp. 46–47.

27

Apparent Magnitude: Apparent Star Brightness

Stars vary widely in brightness. Some appear very bright, while others are barely visible to the naked eye. Around 150 B.C., long before the invention of telescopes, the Greek astronomer Hipparchus devised a scale to measure apparent magnitude, the brightness of stars as seen with the naked eye from Earth. He gave a value of 1 to the brightest star and a value of 6 to the dimmest. Today, we use a variation of his scale to measure the brightness of stars. Instead of observing and estimating magnitudes with the naked eye, we now use an instrument called a photometer, which produces more precise measurements. Also, the scale has been extended beyond 1 to 6 so astronomers can measure an even broader range of brightness.

In this project, you will demonstrate the effect of luminosity and distance on the apparent magnitude of a star. You will build an instrument to measure apparent magnitude. You will also learn how apparent magnitude differs from intrinsic (natural) luminosity, which is the amount of light a star emits. You will discover the difference between apparent and absolute magnitude.

Getting Started

Purpose: To demonstrate how distance affects the brightness of an object.

Materials

3 pencils

yardstick (meterstick)

2 identical incandescent flashlights with new batteries

2 helpers

Procedure

1. In an open area outdoors, stick a pencil in the ground to mark the starting point. Use the yardstick (meterstick) to measure two distances from the pencil, one at 10 feet (3 m) and the second at 30 feet (9 m). Mark these distances with pencils in the ground.

2. At night, stand beside the first pencil.

3. Ask your helpers to hold flashlights and to stand side by side at the second pencil, 10 feet (3 m) away.

4. Instruct your helpers to turn on their flashlights and shine them toward you.

5. Look at the lights just long enough to compare their brightness.

6. Ask one of your helpers to move to the third pencil, 30 feet (9 m) away, while continuing to shine the light toward you (see Figure 27.1).

7. Again, compare the brightness of the lights.

8. Ask your other helper to move to the third pencil while continuing to shine the light toward you.

9. As before, compare the brightness of the lights.

Figure 27.1

Results

The lights appear equally bright at an equal distance from you. When they are at different distances, the closer light appears brighter.

Why?

Magnitude is a measure of how bright a celestial body appears to be. **Apparent magnitude** is a measure of how bright a celestial body appears as viewed with the naked eye from Earth. Apparent magnitudes are ranked on a **magnitude scale,** with an inverse relation between brightness and magnitude numbers, expressed as magnitudes. For example, the magnitude 1 star in Figure 27.2 is brighter than the magnitude 3 star. Apparent magnitude is not a measure of luminosity. A star's **luminosity** is the amount of light energy it gives off in a given amount of time. When stars have the same luminosity, the closer star, like the closer flashlight, appears brighter.

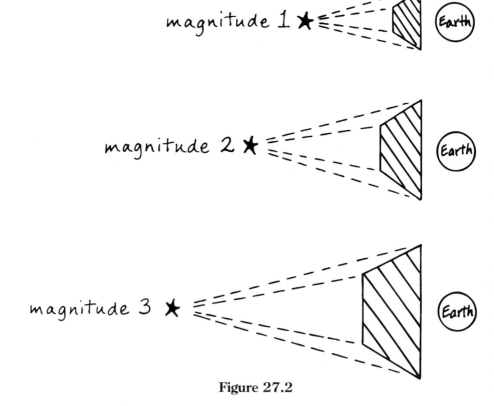

Figure 27.2

Try New Approaches

The star Aldebaran, in the constellation Taurus, is about 50 times larger and about 100 times more luminous than the Sun. It appears far less bright, however, because it is so far away from Earth. Demonstrate how distance affects the apparent magnitude of stars with unequal luminosity. Repeat the experiment using two flashlights, fresh batteries in one and weak batteries in the other.

Design Your Own Experiment

1. Design a model to illustrate how distance affects the apparent magnitude of stars with equal luminosity. One way is to make a drawing using lines to indicate luminosity. In Figure 27.2, the three stars emit the same amount of energy, as indicated by the number of lines (6) in the boxes. The numbers show, however, that their apparent magnitude varies, with the closest star appearing the brightest (having the lowest magnitude number).

2. Design an experiment to measure the apparent magnitude of stars. One way is to make a brightness viewer. The following steps provide a method for testing the brightness of a magnitude 1 star.

   ▪ Punch two holes near the short edge of an index card. Label the card "Magnitude 1."

   ▪ Cover one of the holes with a piece of transparent (not frosted) tape (see Figure 27.3). The covered hole is the testing hole. The uncovered hole is the viewing hole.

   ▪ To calibrate the viewer:

     (1) Through the viewing hole, look at a star known to be of magnitude 1. For information about star magnitude, see Terence Dickinson, *Night Watch* (Willowdale, Ontario: Firefly Books, 1998), pp. 100–119.

     (2) Look at the same star through the testing hole. The star should be barely visible. If it appears bright, add more layers of tape until the star is barely visible. *Note:* Be careful to keep the layers of tape clean and wrinkle free.

   ▪ To use the viewer, find a star by looking through the viewing hole. Then move the viewer so that you look at the same star through the testing hole. If you can barely see the star, it has a magnitude of 1 or less.

   b. To identify stars with magnitudes greater than 1, repeat the previous experiment for stars of greater magnitude.

Figure 27.3

3. The stars that make up the bowl of the Little Dipper have magnitudes of 2, 3, 4, and 5 (see Figure 27.4). Use these stars as a "magnitude scale in the sky" against which the magnitudes of other stars can be compared and estimated.

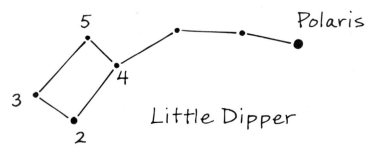

Figure 27.4

Get the Facts

Some stars give off much more light than the Sun, but Earth receives thousands of millions of times as much light from the Sun than from any other star. Why? To compare the light outputs of the Sun and other stars, astronomers use an *absolute magnitude* scale. How was it developed? How does it work? For information, see the *National Audubon Society Field Guide to the Night Sky* (New York: Knopf, 1995), pp. 24–25.

28 Parallax: Apparent Shift of an Object

When an observer changes viewing positions, a nearer object appears to move somewhat in relation to objects in the distant background. Scientists call this apparent movement parallax. Astronomers use parallax to measure the distance of stars.

In this project, you will discover how two factors, the distance from an object and the baseline (distance between observing points), affect parallax. You will learn how to measure the distance to a nearby object using parallax shift. You will also find out how to measure the distance to faraway celestial bodies.

Getting Started

Purpose: To determine how the distance to an object affects parallax.

Materials

marking pen
yardstick (meterstick)
22-by-28-inch (55-by-70-cm) sheet of white poster board
masking tape
7-foot (2.1-m) string
flat toothpick

Procedure

1. Draw 27 lines 1 inch (2.5 cm) apart across the poster board parallel to the short ends. Number the lines from left to right.

2. Tape the poster board to the edge of a table so that the lines run vertically.

3. Measure 14 inches (35 cm) from one end of the string. Place a piece of tape on the string at this point. Label the piece of tape "1."

4. From the tape on the string, measure 1 foot (30 cm) and place a second piece of tape. Label the piece of tape "2." Repeat this step four times, numbering the pieces of tape in order. There should be six pieces of tape on the string.

5. Place the yardstick (meterstick) so that about 6 inches (15 cm) of it extends over the center of the poster board. Tape the measuring stick to the table.

6. Tape the toothpick to the extended end of the measuring stick, pointing down.

7. Lay 2 inches (5 cm) of the end of the string that is near tape 1 on the extended end of the stick. Tape the string to the stick.

8. Sit on the floor in front of the toothpick. Stretch the string and adjust your sitting position so that label 1 touches your nose. In this position, your eyes are in line with and about 1 foot (0.3 m) from the toothpick.

9. Close your left eye and look at the toothpick with your right eye (see Figure 28.1). Move your head until the toothpick aligns with one of the vertical lines on the poster board. Note the number of that line.

10. Without moving your head, open your left eye and close your right eye. Note the number of the line the toothpick appears to move to. If the toothpick falls between lines, estimate the line number to the nearest tenth.

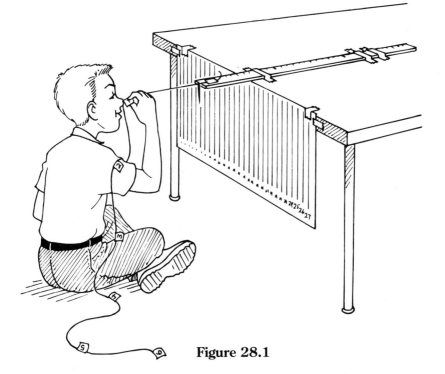

Figure 28.1

11. Record the parallax measurement in a table like Table 28.1. Determine the parallax by finding the difference between the positions of the toothpick as seen with your right and left eyes. For example, if you see the toothpick in front of line 4 with your right eye and in front of line 9 with your left eye, the parallax equals 9 minus 4, or 5 spaces.

12. Repeat steps 8 to 11 at each of the marked distances on the string.

Table 28.1 Parallax Effect			
Distance from the Object, feet (m)	Right Eye Position	Left Eye Position	Parallax, spaces
1 (0.3)	9	4	5
2 (0.6)			
3 (0.9)			
4 (1.2)			
5 (1.5)			
6 (1.8)			

Results

Parallax decreases as distance from the object increases.

Why?

Each eye sees the toothpick from a different point. The distance between the points is the **baseline.** The apparent change in position of an object when viewed from two different points is called **parallax.** As the distance from the toothpick increased, parallax decreased. The farther away an object, the smaller the measurement of parallax.

Try New Approaches

How does the length of the baseline affect parallax? Look in a mirror and measure the distance between the pupils of your eyes. This was the baseline for the original experiment. Make a viewer with baselines greater and less than your eye baseline. Draw a 5-inch (12.5-cm) line across the widest part of a 4-by-6-inch (10-by-15-cm) index card. Punch a hole at each end of the line. Label each hole "1." In the center of the card, punch two holes 1 inch (2.5 cm) apart and label each hole "2." Repeat the experiment twice, first looking through the number 1 holes, then through the number 2 holes. To look through the holes, begin by holding the card so that its center is in line with the end of your nose. Keeping the card in place, move your head to the right and left to look through the holes.

Design Your Own Experiment

1. Design an experiment to demonstrate how parallax effect is used to measure the distance (d) to a nearby object. One way is to use a predetermined baseline and measure the parallax shift. Then determine the distance to the object using the following equation:

$$d = 57.3° \text{ (baseline distance} \div \text{parallax shift)}$$

   Note: This equation yields a number without a unit of measurement. When no unit of measurement is indicated in giving the measure of an angle, the angle is understood to be expressed in radians. To express the angle in degrees, the conversion 57.3° per 1 radian is used.

   Mark two points on the ground exactly 10 feet (3 m) apart and about 30 paces from a tree. Label the points "A" and "B." Stand at point A and use a cross-staff to measure the angular separation between the tree and a distant object such as a telephone pole. (See Chapter 2 for more information about angular separation and using a cross-staff to measure it.) *Note:* The distant object (telephone pole) should be about 10 times or more distant than the near object (tree) whose distance is being measured. Move to point B and make another measurement (see Figure 28.2). For the example shown, if the angular separation measures 5° from point A and 5° from point B, then the parallax shift equals their sum, or 10°. The distance to the tree is then calculated as follows:

$$d = 57.3° \text{ (10 feet} \div 10°) \text{ or } 57.3° \text{ (3 m} \div 10°)$$
$$= 57.3 \text{ feet (17.2 m)}$$

From point A

From point B

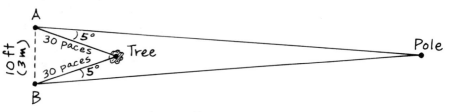

Figure 28.2

b. Use a tape measure to measure the distance to the tree. Then use the method in Appendix 2 to determine the relative error of your measurements. This will give you an indication of how accurate your cross-staff is.

2. Diagram the parallax shift of a star using the diameter of Earth's orbit as the baseline. For information as well as other parallax experiments, see *Janice VanCleave's A+ Projects in Earth Science* (New York: Wiley, 1999), pp. 43–50.

Get the Facts

The parallax method cannot measure the distance of most stars because they are too far away. Instead, astronomers use *photometers* (light meters), *Cepheids* (pulsating stars), and, for stars in remote galaxies, something called red shift. For information on how these methods are used to calculate distances to stars, see Terence Dickinson, *Nightwatch: A Practical Guide to Viewing the Universe* (Willowdale, Ontario: Firefly Books, 1998), p. 89.

PART VII

Meteors and Artificial Satellites

29 Meteors: Streaks of Light in the Sky

What are those points of light moving across the sky? If they blink or glow red, they are probably an airplane. A white, continuous, slowly moving light is probably an artificial satellite. The bright streaking white light of a "shooting star" is actually a meteor.

In this project, you will model the plane of Earth's orbit in relation to that of a comet, which is a celestial body with an extremely elongated orbit about the Sun. You will discover the two types of meteoroid streams and learn how to represent them. You will also compare the number of meteors in "showers" with the number of meteors that fall to Earth sporadically.

Getting Started

Purpose: To model Earth's orbit passing through a comet's orbit.

Materials

pen
1-by-3-inch (2.5-by-7.5-cm) strip of poster board
one-hole paper punch
three 12-inch (30-cm) pipe cleaners—2 yellow, 1 green

Procedure

1. Draw the Sun in the center of the strip of poster board.

2. Punch four holes in the strip, centering them near the edges of the four ends.

3. Thread the green pipe cleaner through the holes on the short ends of the strip. Twist its ends together, and form it into an elliptical shape. This is a model of Earth's orbit.

4. Twist the ends of the yellow pipe cleaners together to form one long piece. Thread it through the remaining holes. Twist the ends together and form it into an ellipse. This is a model of a comet's orbit.

5. Position the two orbits at angles so that Earth's orbit touches the comet's orbit at only one point (see Figure 29.1).

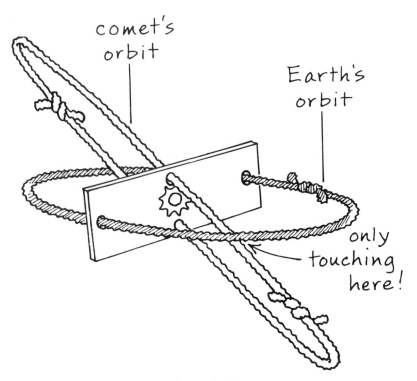

comet's
orbit

Earth's
orbit

only
touching
here!

Figure 29.1

Results

The comet's orbit is at an angle nearly perpendicular to Earth's orbit, so they only touch at one point.

Why?

Comets are celestial bodies made of dust, rock, sand, gases, and ices (mainly water and carbon dioxide) that move in an extremely elongated orbit about the Sun. They are often called "dirty snowballs." When they get near the inner planets, the Sun's heat vaporizes surface ice, freeing some of the rock, sand, and dust. These pieces become meteoroids, scattered along the comet's path. Meteoroids from comets are generally the size of dust specks, while those from **asteroids** (irregularly shaped rocky chunks of matter that rotate as they orbit the Sun, generally between Mars and Jupiter) can be very large.

When a meteoroid enters Earth's atmosphere, it and the light it emits are called a **meteor**. Meteors move so fast that friction with the air causes them to heat up and vaporize. The hot vapor is incandescent. This incandescence is the light of a "shooting star." Any meteor large enough to survive its fall through Earth's atmosphere and actually make it to Earth's surface is called a meteorite.

The orbit of Earth and the orbits of most comets never meet. But some comets have orbital paths that do intersect with Earth's orbit. Thus, in its annual trip around the Sun, Earth passes through the orbital paths of several comets at different times throughout the year. Each time this happens, Earth passes through debris the comet left in its path, and a **meteor shower** (increase in the number of observed meteors) is seen by observers on Earth.

Try New Approaches

Since comets approach the Sun from all directions, most of them are on a different orbital plane than Earth. Therefore, Earth passes through the path of any given comet only once each year. However, it is possible for Earth to intersect a comet's path twice each year—once where the comet is coming in toward the Sun, and again when it is heading back out away from the Sun. This is the case with the famous Comet Halley, which happens to have an orbital plane similar to Earth's. It produces two annual meteor showers: the Eta Aquarids in May and the Orionids in October. Model this by repeating the experiment, making the four holes in line with one another, with two holes on each side of the Sun.

Design Your Own Experiment

1a. Most meteors are sporadic. The remains of a long-dead comet are spread widely across space, coming from any and all directions. Design an experiment that compares the number of meteors in a shower to the numbers that come sporadically during a given time period. Make nightly counts during a meteor shower. Do the same when the meteor fall is sporadic. For information about how to observe and count meteors, as well as dates of expected meteor showers, see Fred Schaaf, *40 Nights to Knowing the Sky* (New York: Holt, 1998), pp. 120–127.

b. The meteoroids of a meteor shower are part of a **meteoroid stream** (debris from a comet traveling in or near a comet's orbital path). These meteoroids may be bunched, or concentrated, in one part of the comet's orbit. When Earth passes through such a bunched swarm of meteoroids, observers on Earth are likely to see a **meteor storm** (many meteors occurring in a short period of time). Or the meteoroids may be rather uniformly distributed along a comet's path. This occurs when comets have made many trips around the Sun, and generally produces more sparse meteor showers. Design a display for these two types of meteoroid streams.

Get the Facts

Meteors sometimes leave a glowing trail across the sky called a *meteor train*. What causes this trail? How long does it last? For information about meteor trains and other types of meteors, such as fireballs and bolides, see Schaaf, *40 Nights,* pp. 118–120.

A natural satellite is a celestial body that orbits another, such as the Moon, which orbits Earth. An artificial satellite is a man-made object that orbits Earth. Artificial satellites are raised to a desired height above Earth and launched by rockets parallel to Earth's surface. This forward velocity and the force of gravity keep the satellite in orbit around Earth.

In this project, you will learn about launching speed and its effect on a man-made satellite's orbit. You will discover the best times to see satellites and how to measure their angular velocity. You will also find out why satellites are launched in different directions.

Getting Started

Purpose: To model how a satellite is launched into orbit.

Materials

2 equal-size books, each about 10 inches (25 cm) long

index card

transparent tape

3 rulers—2 must be identical and have a groove down the center

walnut-size piece of modeling clay

bath towel

marble

Procedure

1. Lay the books end to end on a table.

2. Lay the index card on the end of the books farther from the edge of the table.

3. Tape the grooved rulers together end to end. Tape only on the ungrooved side. This is your launcher.

4. Lay the launcher on the books so that one end is on the index card. Raise that end 2 inches (5 cm) above the book. Put the clay under the end for support. Let the other end of the launcher extend over the end of the books.

5. Adjust the books so that the extended end of the launcher is 4 inches (10 cm) from the edge of the table.

6. Lay the towel on the floor near the edge of the table. The towel will help stop the marble when it hits the floor.

7. Position the marble on the raised end of the launcher, then release it (see Figure 30.1). The marble should land on the towel.

8. Observe the path of the marble after it leaves the launcher.

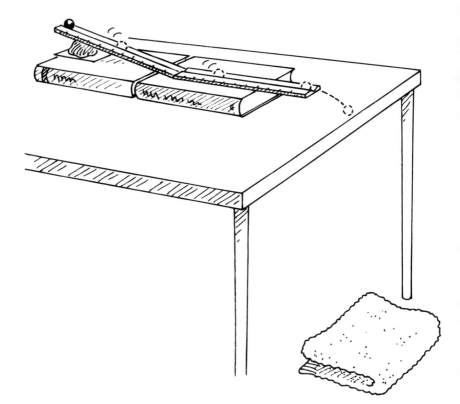

Figure 30.1

Results

The marble's path curves after it leaves the launcher.

Why?

In this model, the table represents Earth. The top of the books is a position above Earth's surface where the "marble satellite" is launched horizontally, parallel to Earth's surface. After it separates from its launcher, the satellite moves in a curved path. The curve results from the satellite's forward horizontal velocity (speed in a specific direction) and the downward pull of gravity. A real satellite would continue in a curved path and return to its launching point.

Try New Approaches

If the horizontal velocity of the marble satellite is great enough, the gravity pulls it into a curved path past the edge of the table. Demonstrate the effect of different horizontal velocities on the path of the satellite by repeating the experiment, raising the end of the launcher to different heights.

Design Your Own Experiment

1a. Earth's surface curves away from a line **tangent** (touching at a single point) to its surface at a rate of $3\frac{3}{50}$ miles (4.9 km) for every 5 miles (8 km). So, near Earth's surface, an object traveling at 5 miles (8 km) per second would maintain its altitude and move in a circular path around Earth. Draw a diagram to represent the effect of launching speeds greater than, less than, and equal to 5 miles (8 km) per second.

b. A satellite's horizontal speed depends on its distance above Earth, which affects the strength of gravity acting on the satellite. The gravity at a certain distance from the center of Earth can be calculated by using this equation:

$$g_1/g_2 = r_2^2/r_1^2$$

where g_1 = 9.8 m/s², gravity at distance equal to the radius of earth (at surface)

r_1 = 12,757 Km, radius of Earth

g_2 = gravity at distance r_2

r_2 = distance from center of Earth to satellite's orbit

The least velocity a satellite must have to orbit Earth is determined by this equation:

$$V = \sqrt{gr}$$

where V = the velocity of the satellite

g = the acceleration of gravity at distance r from the center of Earth

r = the average radius of the satellite's orbit from the center of Earth

Satellites that stay above one place on Earth as they orbit are called **geosynchronous statellites.** These satellites orbit at an altitude of 22,300 miles (13,938 km). Use these formulas to determine the velocity of a geosynchronous satellite and the gravity acting on it. **Science Fair Hint:** Prepare a diagram showing satellites at different distances from Earth's surfaces, the calculations used to determine their velocity, and the gravity acting on them. For more information, look up satellite velocity in a physics text.

2. Satellites look like slow-moving stars. Those in orbits at an altitude of 300 miles (480 km) or less are visible to the naked eye. Determine when satellites are most visible. Observe satellites at different times of the night and during different seasons. For more information on satellite motion, see Terence Dickinson, *Night Watch* (Willowdale, Ontario: Firefly Books, 1999), p. 35.

3. Determine the **angular velocity** (angular displacement per unit time of an object moving in a curved path) of satellites by measuring the angular distance traveled during a measured amount of time. Find out which satellites are visible on a certain date from sources such as *Sky and Telescope* magazine or from websites such as www.skyandtelescope.com. (See Chapter 2, "Angular Separation" for information about measuring angular distance.)

Get the Facts

Most satellites are launched from west to east, but some are launched to orbit Earth from pole to pole. Why is a launch into a polar orbit more difficult? What are satellites used for? For information, see Dinah Moche, *Astronomy Today* (New York: Random House, 1995), pp. 20–21.

Appendix 1

Random Error of Measurement

Purpose: To determine the uncertainty of experimental measurements.

Materials

calculator

Procedure

1. Calculate the average of the measurements. For example, the average of the sample measurements in Table A1.1 is:

$$\text{average} = (28° + 30° + 31° + 29° + 30°) \div 5$$
$$= 29.6°$$

2. Calculate the random error (E) of the average measurement using these steps:

Table A1.1 Angles of Measurements	
Measurement	Angle, °
1	28
2	30
3	31
4	29
5	30

- Calculate the range (R) of the measurements by finding the difference between the largest and smallest measurement values. In Table A1.1, the difference between the largest and smallest measured angles is:

$$R = 30° - 28°$$
$$= 2°$$

- Calculate the random error by dividing the range by $\sqrt{(n-1)}$, where n is the number of measurements. The equation that expresses this is:

$$E = R \div \sqrt{(n-1)}$$

189

For the sample data, the random error would be:

$$E = 2° \div \sqrt{(5-1)}$$
$$= 2° \div \sqrt{4}$$
$$= 2° \div 2$$
$$= 1°$$

- To express the random error of your measurements, you would say that the value of the angle is 29.6° ± 1°. This means that the measurement is between 28.6° and 30.6°.

Appendix 2

Relative Error: Percentage Error

Purpose: To calculate the relative error of experimental measurements.

Materials

calculator

Procedure

1. Calculate the average of the measurements. For example, the average of the sample experimental measurements in Table A2.1 is:

$$\text{average} = (28° + 30° + 31° + 29° + 30°) \div 5$$
$$= 29.6°$$

Table A2.1 Angles of Measurements	
Measurement	Angle, °
1	28
2	30
3	31
4	29
5	30

2. Use the following equation to determine the relative error (also called percentage error) of the measurements. For example, if the accepted (known) value for the angle measurement is 29.8°, the relative error for the experimental measurement would be:

$$E_r = E_a \div A \times 100\%$$

where E_r is the relative error, E_a is the absolute error (the difference between the known and experimental measurements), and A is the known measurement. Note that E_a is the experimental measurement minus the accepted measurement. For this sample, the absolute error is $29.6° - 29.8° = -0.2°$.

$$E_r = -0.2° \div 29.8° \times 100\%$$
$$= -0.67\%$$

The sign of the absolute or relative error merely indicates whether the result is low (–) or high (+).

Appendix 3

Planet Facts and Figures

Planet Facts and Figures							
Celestial Body	Diameter, miles (km)	Average Density g/ml (water = 1)	Albedo	Aphelion or Greatest Distance from Sun, millions of miles (millions of km)	Perihelion or Least Distance from Sun, millions of miles (millions of km)	Average Distance from Sun, millions of miles (millions of km)	Period of Rotation, hours
Mercury	3,047 (4,878)	5.4	0.1	44 (70)	29 (46)	36 (58)	1,407.5
Venus	7,562 (12,100)	5.3	0.76	68 (109)	67 (107)	68 (108)	5,832
Earth	7,973 (12,757)	5.5	0.39	95 (152)	92 (147)	93 (149)	24
Mars	4,247 (6,796)	3.9	0.16	156 (249)	129 (207)	143 (228)	24.6
Jupiter	89,875 (143,800)	1.3	0.52	510 (816)	463 (741)	486 (778)	9.8
Saturn	75,412 (120,660)	0.7	0.61	942 (1,507)	842 (1,347)	892 (1,427)	10.2
Uranus	31,949 (51,118)	1.2	0.35	1,875 (3,000)	1,712 (2,740)	1,794 (2,870)	15.2
Neptune	30,937 (49,500)	1.7	0.35	2,838 (4,540)	2,782 (4,452)	2,810 (4,497)	16
Pluto	1,434 (2,294)	2.0	0.5	4,604 (7,366)	2,771 (4,434)	3,688 (5,900)	153

Appendix 4

Tangent Table

Tangent Table		
Angle	tan	tan
0°	.0000	1.0000
1°	.0175	1.0355
2°	.0349	1.0724
3°	.0524	1.1106
4°	.0699	1.1504
5°	.0875	1.1918
6°	.1051	1.2349
7°	.1228	1.2799
8°	.1405	1.3270
9°	.1584	1.3764
10°	.1763	1.4281
11°	.1944	1.4826
12°	.2126	1.5399
13°	.2309	1.6003
14°	.2493	1.6643
15°	.2679	1.7321
16°	.2867	1.8040
17°	.3057	1.8807
18°	.3249	1.9626
19°	.3443	2.0503
20°	.3640	2.1445
21°	.3839	2.2460
22°	.4040	2.3559
23°	.4245	2.4751
24°	.4452	2.6051
25°	.4663	2.7475
26°	.4877	2.9042
27°	.5095	3.0777
28°	.5317	3.2709
29°	.5543	3.4874
30°	.5774	3.7321
31°	.6009	4.0108
32°	.6249	4.3315
33°	.6494	4.7046
34°	.6745	5.1446
35°	.7002	5.6713
36°	.7265	6.3138
37°	.7536	7.1154
38°	.7813	8.1443
39°	.8098	9.5144
40°	.8391	11.4301
41°	.8693	14.3007
42°	.9004	19.0811
43°	.9325	28.6363
44°	.9657	57.2900
45°	1.0000	∞

Appendix 5
Sources of Scientific Supplies

Catalog Suppliers

Carolina Biological Supply
  Company
2700 York Road
Burlington, NC 27215
(800) 334-5551

Connecticut Valley Biological
  Company
82 Valley Road
P.O. Box 326
Southhampton, MA 01073
(800) 628-7748

Cuisenaire
10 Bank Street
P.O. Box 5026
White Plains, NY 10606
(800) 237-3142

Delta Education, Inc.
P.O. Box 915
Hudson, NH 03051-0915
(800) 258-1302

Fisher Scientific
Educational Materials Division
485 South Frontage Road
Burr Ridge, IL 60521
(708) 655-4410
(800) 766-7000

Frey Scientific Division of
  Beckley Cardy
100 Paragon Parkway
Mansfield, OH 44903
(800) 225-3739

NASCO
901 Janesville Avenue
P.O. Box 901
Fort Atkinson, WI 53538
(800) 677-2960

WWR/Sargent-Welch
911 Commerce Court
Buffalo Grove, IL 60089
(800) 727-4368

Ward's Natural Science
5100 West Henrietta Road
Rochester, NY 14586
(800) 962-2660

Glossary

altazimuth system   In astronomy, a coordinate system used to locate celestial bodies by their altitude and azimuth.

altitude   The angular height of a celestial body above the horizon.

altitude lines   Imaginary parallel circles on the celestial sphere representing angular distances above the horizon.

amplitude   In waves, the height of the crest or trough.

angular diameter   Apparent diameter expressed in radians or degrees.

angular distance   See **angular separation.**

angular separation   Apparent distance expressed in radians or degrees.

angular velocity   The angular displacement per unit time of an object moving in a curved path, expressed in degrees or radians.

aperture   An opening in an optical instrument through which light enters; in a telescope, the diameter of the objective lens or primary mirror.

aphelion   Point in a planet's orbit farthest from the Sun.

apogee   Point in the Moon's or a man-made satellite's orbit farthest from Earth.

apparent diameter   How large an object's diameter appears to be from a specific distance.

apparent distance   How large the linear measurement between two points appears to be.

apparent magnitude   The measure of how bright a celestial body appears as viewed with the naked eye from Earth.

apparent speed   Angular distance per time.

arc   A segment of a circle.

asteroids   Irregularly shaped rocky chunks of matter that rotate as they orbit the Sun, generally between Mars and Jupiter.

astronomical unit (AU)   A unit of measurement used to measure distance in the solar system, based on the average distance between Earth and the Sun.

atmosphere   The blanket of gases surrounding a celestial body; air surrounding Earth.

axis   An imaginary line through a body or the north-to-south line through the center of a celestial body from pole to pole about which the body rotates.

azimuth   The angular distance of a celestial body in degrees clockwise along the horizon from true north.

barycenter   The point between binary bodies where their mass seems to be concentrated and the point about which they rotate.

baseline   The distance between two observing points.

basin   Large craters that are several miles (km) in diameter.

binary bodies   Two celestial bodies held together by mutual gravitational attraction.

binary stars   Double stars that are relatively close to each other and revolve around a common point called the barycenter.

binoculars   An optical instrument somewhat like two small refracting telescopes joined together that magnifies objects viewed from a great distance.

celestial bodies   Natural objects in the sky, such as the Sun, moons, and planets, and stars.

celestial equator   An imaginary circle that divides the celestial sphere in half, is perpendicular to the sphere's axis, and is in line with Earth's equator.

celestial globe   A model of the celestial sphere.

celestial longitude line   See **great circle.**

celestial pole   One of two ends of the axis of the celestial sphere; the points on the celestial sphere in line with the ends of Earth's axis.

celestial sphere   An imaginary sphere that has Earth at its center and all the other celestial bodies scattered around the sphere.

centrifugal force   A force that causes an object turning around a center to move outward from the center.

chromosphere   The layer of the Sun's atmosphere between the photosphere and the corona.

circumpolar stars   Stars that always appear above the horizon and near a celestial pole.

comet   A celestial body made of dust, rock, sand, gases, and ices (mainly water and carbon dioxide) that moves in an extremely elongated orbit about the Sun.

compass rose   A circle marked in degrees that is used to indicate azimuth.

conjunction   The position of celestial bodies when they are on the same celestial longitude line as viewed from Earth.

constellation   A group of stars forming a pattern; a specific part of the sky.

constructive interference   The effect that occurs when the crests and troughs of two overlapping waves match, forming a combined wave of greater amplitude and resulting in brighter light and light bands.

convection zone   The layer of the sun between the radiation zone and the photosphere.

converge   To come together.

coordinates   Two numbers that identify a location.

core   The center of a celestial body such as the Sun.

corona   The outermost layer of the Sun's atmosphere.

crater   A circular depression of any size, usually caused by the impact of a solid body or by a surface eruption.

crest   The top of a wave.

cross-staff   An instrument used to measure angular separation.

dark adapted   Having increased light-gathering power of the eye due to pupil dilation.

declination   The angular distance of a celestial body north or south of the celestial equator.

density   The mass per unit volume of a material.

dependent variable   The part of an investigation that changes in response to the independent variable.

destructive interference   The effect occurs when the crests and troughs of two overlapping waves are opposite, forming a combined wave of less amplitude and resulting in less bright or canceled light, and dark bands.

diffraction   The spreading of light as it passes the edge of an obstacle.

diffraction fringe   The blurred edges of an obstacle due to the diffraction of light as it passes the obstacle's edges.

diurnal circle   The daily circular path of a circumpolar star.

diurnal motion   The apparent daily movement of a celestial body.

double stars   Two stars that appear to be close together.

due north   The direction of Earth's magnetic north pole.

east quadrature   See **quadrature.**

eccentricity   A ratio that describes how much an ellipse deviates from the shape of a perfect circle, calculated by dividing the distance between the foci of the ellipse by the length of its major axis.

eclipsing binary system   Binary stars in which one star periodically moves in front of the other and partially or completely blocks its light.

ecliptic   The Sun's apparent yearly path across the celestial sphere; plane of Earth's orbit.

ellipse   A slightly flattened circle, such as the shape of the orbital path of planets and some satellites.

ellipticity   See **oblateness.**

elongation   The angular separation between the Sun and a planet as viewed from Earth.

equator   An imaginary line running east and west around the middle of a celestial body or the celestial sphere.

equatorial coordinate system   A method of locating celestial bodies by their right ascension and declination.

extrapolate   To make a logical estimate of the next value.

eyepiece   The lens you look through on an optical instrument.

first law of planetary motion   Kepler's law which states that the orbits of the planets around the Sun are ellipses in which the Sun is at one focus.

first quarter   A phase of the Moon when one-half of the side facing Earth is illuminated and is equal to about one-fourth of the Moon's total surface.

focal length   The distance from a lens to the focal point.

focal point   The point where light rays passing through a lens converge (come together).

focus (plural **foci**)   One of two fixed points in an ellipse.

full moon   A phase of the Moon when the side of the Moon facing Earth is completely illuminated.

Galilean satellite   Any of the four largest moons of Jupiter: Io, Europa, Ganymede, and Callisto.

geosynchronous satellite   A man-made satellite that stays above one place on Earth during its orbit.

granulation   The grainy appearance of the Sun's photosphere due to granules.

granule   A bright spot on the Sun's surface that is the top of a rising current of hot gases from the convection zone, measuring about 900 miles (nearly 1,500 km) across.

gravity   A force of attraction between all objects in the universe.

great circle   A circle around a sphere that has the same center point as the sphere.

greatest elongation   The maximum angular separation between the Sun and a planet as viewed from Earth.

highlands   Lighter areas on the Moon caused by regions of higher than average elevation that are the older, cratered region of the Moon's surface and cover more than 70% of the Moon's surface.

high noon   The time of day when the Sun is highest in the sky.

horizon   An imaginary line where the sky appears to touch Earth.

hour circle   A great circle on a celestial globe running from pole to pole perpendicular to the equator; also called celestial longitude lines.

impact crater   A crater made when a meteorite slams into the surface of a celestial body.

independent variable   The part of an investigation that is changed.

inertia   The tendency of an object at rest to remain at rest or an object in motion to continue moving in a straight line unless acted on by an opposing outside force.

inferior conjunction   The position of an inferior planet when it lies between Earth and the Sun.

inferior planets   Planets that are closer to the Sun than is Earth, namely, Venus and Mercury.

intergranular lanes   Dark areas between granules where cooler gases return to the convection zone.

interpolate   To predict results between data points.

Jovian planets   Jupiter and other giant planets that are similar to Jupiter, namely, Saturn, Uranus, and Neptune.

latitude lines   Imaginary parallel circles representing angular distances north and south of the equator of a celestial body or the celestial sphere.

light adapted   Having decreased light-gathering power of the eye due to contraction of the pupil.

light amplification   The process by which objects viewed through an optical instrument appear brighter than when viewed with the unaided eye.

light-gathering power The amount of photons that can be collected by an optical instrument.

longitude lines Imaginary great circles running around a celestial body or the celestial sphere from pole to pole that measure angular distances east and west of a designated 0° line.

luminosity The amount of light energy a star gives off in a given amount of time.

lunar eclipse When Earth's shadow falls on and blocks the light of the Moon.

magnification Enlargement of an image; the ratio of the size of an object's image to the size of the object.

magnifying power The number of times an optical instrument can make the size of an image greater than the actual size of an object.

magnitude A measure of how bright a celestial body appears to be; measure of apparent magnitude.

magnitude scale Numbers indicating the range of apparent magnitudes of celestial bodies; expressed as magnitudes denoting an inverse relation between brightness and magnitude number.

maria (singular, **mare**) Dark spots on the Moon caused by lowlands with an elevation about 2 miles (3.2 km) lower than the rest of the surface and covering about 20% of the Moon's surface.

mean solar time See **standard time.**

mean sun time See **standard time.**

meridian An imaginary drawn from north to south on the celestial sphere and passing through the zenith of the observer.

meteor A meteoroid that enters Earth's atmosphere and burns up; also the light a meteor emits because it is heated to a state of incandescence.

meteorite Any meteor that survives its fall through Earth's atmosphere and makes it to Earth's surface; meteroid that strikes the surface of a celestial body.

meteoroid A solid particle from a celestial body that floats around in space in orbit about the Sun.

meteoroid stream Debris from a comet traveling in or near a comet's orbital path.

meteor shower An increase in the number of meteors observed; occurs when Earth passes through a meteoroid stream.

meteor storm Many meteors occurring in a short period of time.

micron   One micron equals to one-millionth of a meter.

minute of arc   A segment of a circle equal to 1/60 of a degree.

moonrise   When the moon appears to rise above the horizon.

moonset   When the moon appears to sink below the horizon.

new moon   The phase of the Moon when the side of the Moon facing Earth is not illuminated.

node   One of two points where two orbital paths cross.

northern hemisphere   The half of the celestial sphere above or north of the celestial equator. (Capitalized: the region north of Earth's equator.)

nuclear fusion   The combining of the nuclei of atoms, resulting in the release of enormous amounts of radiant energy.

objective   The objective lens of a refractive telescope or the primary mirror of a reflective telescope.

objective lens   The lens of a refracting telescope that faces an observed object and collects the light.

oblateness   The flattening of a spherical body, usually caused by rotation, that accounts for the difference between the equatorial and polar diameters of the sphere; also called **ellipticity.**

oblate spheroid   A sphere that is flattened at the poles and bulges at the equator.

occultation   When a large celestial body passes in front of a smaller one. A special case is the Moon passing across the Sun's disk during what is called a solar eclipse.

opposition   When a superior planet is on the side of Earth opposite the Sun and the planet at an elongation of 180°.

optical double stars   Double stars that are actually far apart and have no true relationship to each other.

optical instrument   A device that increases the power of human vision, such as eyeglasses and contact lenses for viewing objects at close range or binoculars and telescopes for viewing objects at a great distance.

orbit   To move in a curved path about another object; the curved path of one object around another.

orbital period   The time per revolution of a revolving celestial body.

parallax   The apparent change in position of an object when viewed from two different points.

pendulum   A weight that is suspended from a point and is free to swing back and forth.

penumbra   The grayish outer part of a sunspot or of a shadow.

perigee   The orbital point of the Moon or man-made satellite at the least distance from Earth.

perihelion   The point in the orbit of a planet at the least distance from the Sun.

period of rotation   The time it takes a celestial body to turn once on its axis.

phase   One of the repeating apparent forms of the sunlit surface of the Moon or a planet facing Earth.

photon   The smallest particle of light.

photosphere   The layer of the Sun outside the convection zone that is the first layer of the Sun's atmosphere and appears to be the visible surface of the Sun.

planets   Large celestial bodies that orbit a sun.

poles   The ends of the axis of a celestial body.

primary mirror   The mirror of a reflecting telescope that faces an observed object and collects the light.

quadrature   The position of a superior planet when it is at an elongation of 90° east (**east quadrature**) or west (**west quadrature**).

radiation   Energy transferred by waves.

radiation zone   The area outside the core of the Sun.

reflecting telescope   An optical instrument that uses mirrors and lenses to gather light.

refracting telescope   An optical instrument that uses only lenses to gather light.

resolution   Capacity of distinguishing between two separate but adjacent light sources.

resolving power   A measure of resolution; an indication of the clarity of the image produced by an optical instrument due to the amount of diffraction fringe produced by the instrument.

revolve   To move in a curved path about another object.

revolution   One turn around a curved path, such as a planet moving around its orbit.

right ascension   The angular distance of a celestial body east of the vernal equinox to the hour circle of the celestial body.

rotation   The turning of a body on its axis.

satellite   A celestial body or man-made body that revolves about another celestial body, such as a moon or a man-made object about a planet.

scale model   A replica made in proportion to the object it represents.

scientific method   The technique of demonstrating a scientific principle or solving a scientific problem by conducting research, stating a purpose, making a hypothesis, testing the hypothesis through experimentation, and summarizing the results in a conclusion.

season   A regularly recurring period of the year characterized by a specific type of weather. The four seasons are, winter, spring, summer, fall.

second of arc   A segment of a circle equal to 1/60 of a minute of arc, or 1/3600 of a degree.

solar eclipse   When the Moon blocks the light of the Sun.

solar noon   The time of day when the Sun is at its highest altitude and hence casts the shortest shadows.

solar radiation   Radiation given off by the Sun.

solar system   A group of celestial bodies that orbits a star called a sun.

solar time   Time determined by the apparent position of the Sun in the sky, reflecting the apparent change in speed of the Sun during the year; also called **true sun time.**

southern hemisphere   The half of the celestial sphere below or south of the celestial equator. (Capitalized: the region south of Earth's equator.)

spectroscope   A device that breaks light into its component parts.

standard noon   Clock time of 12:00 P.M. (disregarding daylight saving time).

standard time   Clock time (disregarding daylight saving time), based on the average or mean daily distance the Sun travels, which is 1° per day eastward along the ecliptic; also called mean sun time or mean solar time.

sunspots   Large dark spots on the Sun's photosphere.

superior conjunction   The position of an inferior planet when it is on the opposite side of the Sun from Earth.

superior planets   Planets farther from the Sun than Earth is.

synodic month   The time between two successive new moons.

tangent (tan)   In a right triangle, the ratio of the length of the side opposite an acute angle to the length of the angle's adjacent side; touching at a single point.

terminator   The dividing line between the illuminated and nonilluminated areas of the Moon.

terrestrial planets   Earth and other planets that are similar to Earth; namely, Mercury, Venus, and Mars.

third law of planetary motion   Kepler's law which states that the more distant a planet's orbit from the Sun, the greater the planet's period of revolution.

third quarter   A phase of the Moon when one-half of the side facing Earth is illuminated, opposite that of the first quarter phase.

total solar eclipse   An eclipse in which the Moon blocks the view of the Sun from observers on Earth.

transit   When a small celestial body passes in front of a larger one, such as an inferior planet passing across the Sun's disk.

trough   The bottom of a wave.

true north   The direction of Earth's geographic North Pole, which is at the north end of Earth's axis.

true sun time   See **solar time.**

umbra   A dark area, especially the darkest part of a sunspot or of a shadow.

unresolved   Not separated, as light in an optical instrument.

vaporized   Changed to gas.

velocity   Speed of an object in a specific direction.

vernal equinox   The position of the Sun on or about March 21 in the northern hemisphere when it crosses the celestial equator.

visible spectrum   The colors that white light is broken into by diffraction.

waning   Decreasing in illumination.

waves   Periodic disturbances in materials or space which have crests and troughs.

waxing   Growing in illumination.

west quadrature   See **quadrature.**

zodiac   A narrow zone on either side of the ecliptic.

zodiac constellation   The constellations within the zodiac.

Index